Why
George Floyd

The Way of Love

By

UWA UDENSI HUNWICK

Published in the United States of America

ISBN 978-1-956741-71-1 (SC)
ISBN 978-1-958518-00-7 (HC)
ISBN 978-1-958518-01-4 (Ebook)

Uwa Udensi Hunwick Publishing
P.O. Box 732037
9301 Kenton Ave APT. 116,
Skokie, IL 60076, USA
www.stellarliterary.com

Ordering Information and Rights Permission:

Quantity sales. Special discounts might be available on quantity purchases by corporations, associations, and others. For details, contact the publisher at the address above.

For Book Rights Adaptation and other Rights Permission. Call us at toll-free 1-888-945-8513 or send us an email at admin@stellarliterary.com.

CONTENTS

ACKNOWLEDGEMENT

This work is the result of my observations and life long experiences, good and bad, big and small, which have been meticulously explained in indisputable and most inspiring spiritual analogous terms, which clarified the spiritual significance of all human activities whatsoever, in the pursuance of the fulfilment of our lives both Here on earth and in the beyond.

This most empowering and convincing explanation came from a one of a kind spiritual only book titled: "In The Light of Truth - The Grail Message" by Abd-ru-shin - after my many years of seeking and searching for the meaning of life, in all the known denominations of Faiths around me, without success nor conviction! The relief, joy and solutions to all life's problems and challenges it gave me, motivated me to once again try to share the knowledge of our possession of the most powerful Sublime power with which to overcome all the problems of our world in this recent book-"Why George Floyd"!

DEDICATION

I dedicate this work to all mankind in pursuance of true progress, lasting peace, freedom and love for every human being, in the firm belief that we are indisputably capable of changing the course of the loveless and therefore destabilising events now prevalent in our world today. We can do this by summoning and utilising our inherent Power of Love at all levels of our interactions, individually and globally, which has been totally ignored till date, at best misdirected and underestimated for a long time now, all to our detriment, politically and above all, spiritually! I am therefore calling all of us to take action in bringing this about. It is high time!

INTRODUCTION

I am a visual artist, a published dramatist, singer song writer, a retired lecturer in the performing arts and a literary author. I am also the widow of the world renowned professor of African history the late John Owen Hunwick, formerly of Northwestern University, Evanston, Illinois and a mother of three.

I have so far published three works: "Monkey on the Tree", about Apartheid South Africa, "The Love That We Are" sub titled "Our True Identity", and "Why Trump". All of which are about my burning desire to reawaken the expression of our inherent power of Sublime Love that exists in all of Creation for making the world a happy and better place for all mankind! My paintings also mostly of spiritual subjects, hang in many households in the USA.

Two of my staged works "Ogbanje" a cultural Dance Drama on reincarnation and "Day Break in Jubena" a critical Nigerian political Musical expose', represented my country of origin - Nigeria at three International Theatre Festivals in the USA, Brazil, Venezuela and Mexico, in the eighties.

My two other Musicals include "The Black Star" which is about African political identity led by late President Kwame Nkruma of Ghana and "Shogbodile" another critical look at the teething problems of a nation emerging from the assimilated colonial indoctrinations with the tendencies of progression into decadence and corruption!

All my works have one common theme: They all express my never dimming desire to find the real purpose for our existence here on earth, asking the same questions and delving deeply into the naturally available yet seemingly illusive answers that stare us all in the face but are simply ignored by the generality of humanity time after time! These questions which I consider crucial to helping mankind come to grips with our common fate are:

Who am I?

What am I doing here? What is this place and,

How am I really to live in this place called the earth?

These questions may seem enigmatic, especially when one tries to relate them to one's own life experiences now climaxed by events in one's corner of the earth; such as many of the kind that has led to George Floyd's murder! In the light of what happened to him that prompted so much outrage and condemning reactions round the planet, one then asks the above questions about him in order to answer those enigmatic existential question about oneself ! Their answers will go along way to making us understand the whys and wherefores of the mechanism of the power that is in operation beyond our sights but is in total control of our lives. It will also shed light to what is required of all of us as human *spirits*!

—

So, who was George Floyd really? What was he doing on earth as a human spirit? How was he supposed to have lived and expect others to do? These questions which critically relate to us will be answered in the body of this work.

PREFACE

In this work, all what I am going to say is an expression of my perceptions of the reasons why on the whole, we are all living a most dysfunctional and unsatisfactory spiritual lives in the world today, offering suggestions for a viable reversal of the dire upheavals this has persistently caused in all aspects of human existence in the past and in the present! This is prompted by my life time of 84 years so far, beginning from my 9th year of life; of the observations of happenings in my community and country, and round the world up till the present time, that have adversely affected humanity's ability to achieving any sustainable degree of peaceful coexistence with one another; exemplified and climaxed by what happened to George Floyd and his likes here and in all the world's villages, towns, cities, and countries!

This sad condition is currently most evident in the prevailing volatile and controversial happenings both here in the USA, in my original home in Nigeria and other parts of Africa, and the world in general; signalling that we must all seriously resolve to take urgent remedial steps to turn things around: So we may escape from the reciprocal repercussions for the ignoble parts we all have played in the destabilisation and dehumanisation of members of our human societies in the universal Divine scheme of Love!

Natural Signs

I'll begin by asking the following pungent questions which the body of the work will try to help us all answer in the different chapters, with the sole aim of helping us all understand the real reason we humans are on earth!—

Why you?

Why me?

Why your parents

Why my parents?

Why your sister?

Why my sister?

Why your brother?

Why my brother?

Why your uncle?

Why my uncle?

Why your auntie?

Why my auntie?

Why your country?

Why my country?

Why the people of the earth?

Why white?

Why black?

Why variegated hues?

Why good?

Why not good?

Why happy?

Why sad?

Why cry?

Why laugh?

Why rich?

Why not rich?

Why strong?

Why weak?

Why tall?

Why not tall?

Why medium?

Why short?

Why free?

Why not free?

Why capable?

Why not capable?

Why Life?

Why Death

Why Spiritual?

Why Physical?

Why Love?

Why George Floyd?

To try and answer these questions myself, I will begin by saying that it is said that experience is the best teacher. That being so, let us all then fall back on our experiences with the natural happenings in our lives and in our environments. There, we will not fail to find out that there are abundant clues all around and within us for discovering the hidden truth about ourselves, as exemplified even in George Floyd. All we need to do, is to stop and contemplate deeply about the results of our own individual actions daily: And the well-structured reactions to these that manifest in the workings of the primordial natural laws that govern creation (whether we know it or not) in the adamantine and all Holy Will of The Creator will be revealed to us!

For instance, we know for a fact, that every act of ours gives us back a pleasant or none pleasant, satisfactory or none satisfactory result. There is simply nothing that does not bear fruit nor have a purpose in our lives! All the elements above and bellow and all so-called inanimate and animate objects including the sand, the stones and insects, play their own parts as they serve their special purposes. The organs of our bodies serve specific purposes in our lives and so even do the names we bear from life time to life time, which serve the special purpose of *supporting* and directing us by their meanings!

This supportive essential power of names is clearly exemplified in the authorship of the special spiritual work, upon whose verifiable "Truth" I base my understanding of life, as *demonstrated* daily and hourly in and around me, and continuously *influence* my undertakings as said. Experience being the best teacher therefore, I now hope to share what I have learnt about Creation and how it works and what part you and I and of course George Floyd are meant to have been playing in making our world a better place, since we all first incarnated on earth eons of spiritual developmental years ago!

For instance, the spiritual one of a kind work says one's name is truly what one really is in this process.Unequivocally indicating the fact that He the Bringer of this work : *"In The Light of Truth- The Grail Message" by Abd-ru-shin,* which is a pen-name now, but the real name He actually bore some three thousand years ago, when He first incarnated in Persia bearing the name- Abd-ru-shin, which means "Son of Light", imbued His work with His essence of *Divine Light,* making every sentence in His Message, written in the Holy Will of His heavenly Father, our God, to shine *"Pure Light"* into the spirit of man; for the comprehensive understanding of all aspects of life and existence in His Father's, our God's Creation.

In that process, He clarified all Biblical and other religious inferences about Creation and misguided *human* interpretations of the Divine phenomenon. Metaphorically put, He shone *"Light"*into the darkness we created and roam about in our world; *spiritually blindfolded* by our none-compliance to His Father's adamantine All-Holy Will! Explained all never before understood or misinterpreted natural phenomena of life and death, birth and rebirth- reincarnation and more; offering indisputable and verifiable truths about whatever the matter may be!

All to enable humanity to finally get rid of the darkness that has enveloped the world throughout history from the radiations of our thoughts, words and our actions and return our world to what it was meant to be, namely a true reflection of Paradise; where only Love and Light reign in the inviolable Will of the Creator! —

*This work *"In the Light of Truth-The Grail Message"* by *Abd-ru-shin* can be obtained from Alexander Bernhardt Publishing. USA.website: http.//www.elaxander-bernhardt.us/

In this spiritual work, the only one of its kind in existence which gives all the answers to all matters of life and existence in relation to the Creator, in all the latent universes known and unknown, visible and invisible, we can be guided to find out what must have led to George Floyd, whose root meaning of the name *George* is "farmer": which biologically connotes the nurturing and preservation of the ecosystem in general, dying as he did. This will throw a glaring Light to our individual plights in the eternal drama of our overall existence!

My own name, being Uwa (Igbo) which means *'the world'* or 'the universe' and better still, *'fate'*; has riddled me with much concern about my life and that of humanity at large in my "*world*" as it were, since childhood! It has compelled me to engage myself in the effort spiritually and artistically to find out what life is all about and to come to understand who we really are, leading to my writing of the work entitled "The Love That We Are" subtitled "Our True Identity", and the other two mentioned earlier, and to the composition of the contents of all of my paintings, songs and poems and finally to this present effort about us and George Floyd!

When you find out the meaning of your name, you will find out how you have been unconsciously struggling to fulfil its directions and perhaps recognise what has been militating or perchance enabling you in your efforts to achieve your spiritual purpose on earth too!

Uwa Udensi Hunwick

The Bad Seeds We Have Sown!

Troubled everyday by all the sad events all around, the voice inside you and I is now crying, knowing that no one is listening to you nor to his or her own conscience anymore!…For this situation to be arrested, we must awaken from our trancelike self- complacency, to do that which will help relieve us from the despair which has wrung our hearts these many gruesome years: turning us into a humanity beleaguered with a prolonged mortal combat with the unrelenting onslaught of an elusive foe! This foe created by us, is so strong that it has numbed our senses, and its pain has spiritually and physically maimed us, leaving us spiritually dead!

We have therefore been sowing bad seeds in Creation in this inertia, mainly because of the *lack* of the necessary fundamental understanding of the necessity of our *spiritual* evolution into higher spirit beings; by achieving spiritual maturity only, through our loving one another unconditionally! If we could but grasp the warnings from our pasts, as George Floyd as a human spirit must have most certainly done, our said nefarious pasts, which unequivocally indicate our consequent future that now looms glaringly over us; we would all resolutely want to rescue humanity from the impending annihilation to which our continued indifference is leading us! That, is what the hero in this book, George Floyd, "spiritually" wanted to help us do by the nature of his death!

At present, we are all dazed, afraid, and flabbergasted and even incoherent when someone asks us what we think or what we conjecture will happen to us in the near future, seeing how generally unpleasant things are right now, with continued events which most times leave us wide-eyed and tongue-tied in our embarrassments and disbelief ! These repeated life's breaches will without any doubt, catapult mankind out of all the so much touted progress that we have made, of apparent unparalleled technological advancements made possible by our global economic achievements, primarily geared towards the enhancement of our comfort and seaming maintenance of peace and material wealth, without any consideration of our *spiritual* welfare; will certainly throw us back into the despondency of a humanity that continues to live by fear and hatred of one another, instead of the much needed expression of sublime "unconditional Love" for one another!

Right now, the daily news is *froth* with agitations and castigations against Tom, Dick and Harry. Stones are regularly being thrown at innocent citizens, countries are waging unnecessary wars all round the globe; without taking good looks at the rank and file of their own ruling citizenry for clues for their endemic social and economic maladies: the West *blaming* the East and the East, the Western world, the so called "New world" pointing threatening fingers at the so called "Old world" and vice-versa; the rich blaming the poor and the poor the rich, the white *blaming* the black and the black and coloured blaming the white! It goes on and on and on!

Despite all the above woes and looming catastrophes these may bring in our " *reaping what we have sown*", we can avert the gruesome repercussions by routing out their root causes to secure for us a better fate! Here is how we would be able to do it. But before we go to the how, we need to know how George Floyd of all people, comes to feature in this monumental cosmic event of humanity at large. —

We all feature in this event in one way or another, because everyone on this planet has something important to contribute in the upbuilding process towards our mutual spiritual as well as material progress in the long run! No one is dispensable in this Divine universal scheme, otherwise humanity would have been made up of clones of each other and all finger prints would have been identical for easy replacement!

It is not in vain therefore, that glaring distinguishing features are present in every family on earth for the character differentiations of their members: a brother may be more predisposed to anger than his siblings and another may be gentle and easy going, another pensive and quarrelsome; another member can be more physically appealing while another is not, another giving, another gifted in the arts etc., etc. All of which are to be of benefit for the whole of humanity and must not be ignored, suppressed or abused but spiritually guided for our spiritual maturity in the upbuilding of Creation. A lot of times however, we suppress, envy or sabotage each other; sowing seeds of resentment, jealousy and the evil tendencies of revenge and worse!

Members of the same family can all have the same gifts but each is meant to expresses it differently and excel differently in specific areas. All are equally meant to transform and channel their different dispositions and gifts into up-building acts that will enable them achieve the same spiritual only goal for which they incarnated on earth! —

George Floyd may have in this case, played his own chosen special role. What about us, the other members of our global family?

Reincarnation

Why can't you be like your sister or your brother? These are questions often asked by the overstressed parent mother or father. The answers to such questions and numerous others for beleaguered mankind, not only about family oriented problems, but also that of all humanity's unsolved spiritual and material chaos, inherent in the world's societal, educational, cultural and political establishments, to the catastrophic level it has risen now; have been undeniably enunciated and explained in all simplicity in the aforementioned only provable and reliable spiritual exposition ever written!

It not only elaborates and explains the presumed mysteries transmitted in the Bible, but dissects the Divine mechanisms in the running of Creation, leading one to the understanding of the truths or misinformations of all religious tenets which have brought varied burdensome misrepresentations of the Godhead in their doctrinal practices; and have led to untold miseries of tortures, and so called "holy wars" such as the Crusades, Jihads, and others, applicable in the perpetration of terrorisms, suicide bombing and Boko Haram of all descriptions!

It also gives lucid spiritual guiding principles for the eradication of all spiritual malpractices of all mankind, irrespective of location, religion, race, education, social or economic status, or ethnicity. In addition, It confirms and bears witness to the fact that we "*Reincarnate*"! A subject that directly relates to the problems discussed in this book with reference to George Floyd as someone who reincarnated just as we have all done several times!

Reincarnation is an important determining factor of our plights in our continued existence on earth, which we do not understand nor take into any consideration in whatever we do, but which greatly impacts our fates in our present lives!

The authorship of the unique book : "In The Light Of Truth-The Grail Message" by Abd-ru-shin, as said earlier, stands as a testimony of the work of the "*reincarnated*" original *"Holy Spirit"* The name Abd-ru-shin is a name taken from the one which He bore in His previous incarnation over three thousand years ago as said, in Persia!

In the said book He categorically gives validity to the spiritual "*truth*" about reincarnation which is one of the *very important* and indisputable aspects of all human existence which have not yet been understood, but which make very critical impacts in our lives! He did this in His present capacity as the "*reincarnated*" Abd-ru-shin , three thousand years ago as said, after His first incarnation on earth, in Persia where in the same manner as at this time, He was given the appointed Holy task by His Father, the Creator Almighty God, to assume the human flesh through birth as Jesus also did two thousand years ago in the same love based dispensation of their Father, our God: for the same purpose of piloting stubborn stumbling mankind to the true knowledge and compliance to the guidance of the love based primordial natural laws of existence, meant only to lead mankind to the achievement of their only purpose on earth, which is the development of spiritual consciousness for the attainment of spiritual maturity! This time however it was the last intervention before the judgement as was long prophesied as the "End Time"!

This periodic monumental spiritual occurrence is permitted to take place when humanity is steeped in either idol worshipping, self glorification and lack of true spiritual knowledge, or all combined; further aggravated by materiality, immorality and decadence of the present time; which always prevent mankind from achieving the purpose for which He, our God permitted us to incarnate on earth. This time however, it is the final opportunity in the cosmic cycle of events!—

We have the last chance at this Cosmic turning Point, to obey God's directives of loving others as we consistently love ourselves, and do to them as we would like it be done to us! This is very clearly enunciated in the Living Words of Jesus Christ and again in the Grail Message, which is *also The Living Message of God's relentless Love*, that is none doctrinal. This time however, the Divine message is not only personally written by the said author in living time, but is also undiluted or tampered with in anyway by any human hand or mind with any of the misrepresentations that abound in many religions.

Very much unlike the posthumous hear-say but well meaning biblical documentation of the mission of our Lord Jesus Christ two thousand years ago! This time however, the bringer of the one of a kind holy message emphasises the fact that we have little or no time left to see that we strive in every thing we say, think or do, to comply with God's All-Holy Will lest we'll be finally cast out and be denied any further existence in God's Creation!

That's why it is said to be *"The End Time"* as was once prophesied.

That is why as a last resort, He was once again sent from the Divine Sphere as the Holy Ghost that Jesus had promised mankind would come to judge us of sin and righteousness and in doing so rescue us from our overarching self-complacent obsessions in the idol worship of materiality, intellectual domination and money only oriented pursuits; all of which have left us staggering under the death dealing blow of everlasting spiritual suicide, even after the painful sacrificial reorienting mission of supreme sublime Love of our Lord Jesus Christ in the two thousand years interim.

He, Abd-ru-shin being the reincarnated "Holy Spirit" and the source of our spiritual ego can *never* die! This is why our spirits derived from His everlasting spiritual essence as said earlier also never die, but "reincarnate"!

The knowledge of reincarnation throws open all the shut doors of human understanding of their lives, because it explains all the puzzling questions about the whys and wherefores apparently unexpected and unpleasant things happen to people as it did to George Floyd.—

More Proofs of Reincarnation.

At about seven or eight years old, I asked my step mother why her younger brother breathed noisily and with apparent difficulty even though he was not suffering from any form of cold. She did not hesitate in telling me that the brother told their parents when he began to speak as a toddler, that he will never go to prison again! She further disclosed that an uncle had died in prison and was apparently roughly stuffed into the ground as was the practice with disreputable prisoners in the area in the past. So in the present incarnation, he bore the imprint of that previous treatment as a subconscious yet physical reminder of what he must now avoid doing!

Drawing further from my personal experiences as the best teacher in life and about life, I also want to cite the next testimony of reincarnation which is here supplied by my own grandson Johny, who is now fifteen. When he was only four years old, he said the following to his dad, I quote: "When I was your age, I used to own a farm". At the time his dad who is my son, was in his very early thirties! His mom confirms this happening. He has forgotten it all as we all are known to do as we grow up!

There are also numerous television documentaries of evidences of reincarnations round the world which is available on youtube for anyone to explore for one's education about this truth of our existence. Some of these documentaries can be found in the National Geographic Documentary by Dr. Keith Parson, Scientific Evidence for Reincarnation by Dr. Ian Stevens, Larry King's interview of Dr. E Ben Alexander on reincarnation, and numerous other confirmations also cited there in. I am sure the reader may remember similar anecdotes related by relatives or acquaintances which were simply *brushed* aside!

These are eye openers to the story that now seeks to be fully examined for the revelation of yet another aspect of reincarnation not yet taken into account because of its *grave* implications as evidenced in the murder of Martin Luther King and others before him, now *crowned* with the dastardly murder of George Floyd! This will go along way to enabling us answer the question about who George Floyd *really* was and what he came to do in this incarnation, which will shine light to the other form of reincarnations that are undertaken sometimes by certain types of people!

Mission Karma!

Everyone is familiar with the knowledge of the operation of Karma in our lives, which is the working out of the law of *What you sow you must reap!* (What goes around comes around.) Mankind is however not familiar with what has been finally *revealed* in the aforementioned one of a kind only spiritual book about the *"MISSION KARMA"*—

While in its familiar operation, karma is meant for unconscious but necessary atonement for our misdeeds in previous lives, the *"Mission Karma"* on the other hand, is not for the atonement of any previously committed wrongs in a previous life; but a *"voluntary"* undertaking of any human spirit for the *sole* purpose of giving *selfless help* to other fellow human spirits in a particular earth life, for their advancement to spiritual maturity which is the sole purpose for all human existence! Hence the previous undertakings of heroes like Martin Luther King for our human rights, Rosa Park and many others of different races, in our historic march towards political, social and above all our spiritual emancipation; now very much superseded in its unforgettable gruesomeness by George Floyd's murder in our own life time! —

Speaking about "Mission Karma" the author reveals the never before mentioned phenomenon in these words, I quote: "The case is different where a soul volunteers to undertake a mission, either to help some particular persons or to engage with others in some benevolent work for all mankind. Out of its own free will that soul then accepts in advance all that will happen to it on earth."

The author further says that—"Into families with hereditary diseases souls will be incarnated which, through the reciprocal action, need these diseases for redemption, for purification, or for advancement"—

Jesus Christ on hinting on the subject once asked His disciples who they believed He was. Some said that He was Elijah who had *come back*, others claimed He was one or some other past personages who *had lived before*. He did not disapprove of their beliefs which was normal in the spiritual understanding of that time!

However, the knowledge of reincarnation chronicled in the original bible of the vulgate was later expunged during the reign of Emperor Constantine of historic Constantinople in one of the councils of Nicaea in the 4th A.D., at the request of an influential female patron of the new church formed by the conqueror of the then Byzantine empire!

Nevertheless, the fact that all humanity believes in reincarnation in one form or another, points to the validity of the residual collective memory of all human beings which defies scientific, religious or intellectual certifications, because both are not interchangeable nor interrelated. The intellect which is the basis of science, cannot decipher nor grapple with anything of sublime spiritual import and essence! That is the reason why the scientific or materially oriented human spirit has become incapable of thinking about let alone accepting the truth about spiritual realities! —

Since we have decidedly put the cart before the horse, by cultivating our *intellectual* prowess, raising it to the sagacious prominence of the *decision* maker and our "*blinding*" faith as a decisive spiritual blocker; we have rendered ourselves virtually *impotent* in the management of all our potential sublime spiritual powers for true success as human *spiritual only* tenants on earth! Hence humanity is now labouring in delusion and in vain, despite all their material, theological, technological and scientific superlative achievements and above all, their professed "Faiths"! Because these don't count where the real purpose of the human "*spirit*" is concerned!

Therefore our only salvation from the continuous ominous regression of human spiritual progress lies only in the understanding of the *reality* of the spirit that dwells in each and everyone of us, which is created only to aspire to develop into true "Likenesses of the Image of God". We should not forget that in the beginning The Creator is reported to have said the following: "Let us make man in our own image", meaning in His spiritual essence because

He is unsubstantiated, does not have a physical body. We can only achieve this likenesses by living our lives by expressing the Sublime love that is identical with His, and with which He made us to all living creatures on earth, which events like that of George Floyd's encounter with the Law enforcement personnels should have prompted!

It is gratifying to note that most of the world responded with *their* spontaneous show of Love in their disapproval and condemnation of that which happened on that day! That is not enough at this time however, because judging by the practical outcome of all our agitations and outcries round the world, much is yet to be done, for the awakening of our inner consciousness to the true implementation of the *spiritual* only solution: based on the harness and practical application of the indispensable power of our inherent sublime love energy, which *alone* can counter the overwhelming proclivity to the resort of menacing and destructive agents rather than inspirationally constructive ones for our spiritual upbuilding that leads to the achievement of our prescribed spiritually only acceptable purpose for incarnation! Let us now try to do this by delving into the implications of being a human spirit in the first place!

Who We Really Are

Let us now examine ourselves individually to see what we are geared up to do in the world in order to grapple with the surrounding circumstances of the day to day happenings in our lives, irrespective of our religious persuasions, scientific and academics achievements and material acquisitions or the lack of them all. To do this, there are fundamental pieces of knowledge of existence that we need to have to guide us. This is because just as an auto-salesman recommends a vehicle by identifying its make and capabilities for the driver's satisfaction: we owe it to ourselves to be well acquainted with our makeup and capabilities both physically and above all spiritually for our purpose on earth!

In my understanding of the above, from the indispensable aforementioned one of a kind necessary spiritual revelations in the said book : *We are "spirits" and nothing but spirits,* sojourning on earth for a purpose which has *nothing* to do with power, material acquisitions nor fame! Our individual only purpose on this earth is *the development* of the spirit to *full maturity as a conscious Loving spiritual entity* in human form. It has to do this by interacting with other human spirits and creatures of nature, to enhance its own ennoblement and that of the earth and all that there is in it, for the ultimate replication of its heavenly home of nothing but Sublime *Love!—*

This can never be attained by all our materially sourced and physically directed pursuits, nor all the doctrinal assumptions in the world! Because as spirits we do not originate from the material or physical world nor from that of all the scientific theories, imaginations and inventions; but from the *"spiritual" life giving Force Itself - God !* Without Him, nothing can exist anywhere in the whole universe!

The origination occurred in the outpouring of the creative Divine power of infinite perfection, when at the beginning of creation God gave the fiat : *"Let there be light"* out of His Divine surging and bellowing un-embodied ocean of light flames, which then leapt over the vast boundary of Its Devine realm and bellowed into the void (giving birth to the scientist's conjecture of the"Big Bang") theory! The release of power in the fiat, imbued with all *formative* forces and precision, instantaneously manifested substantive embodied series of hierarchic species of entities; who symbiotically exist within the force in spheres that are at unimaginable distances below the Divine sphere, and where all acts are automatically manifested spiritually to guide all that further manifested below and still manifest in the visible and subsequently manifested physical worlds! Hence, the spiritual always governs all what is just physical; which only serves as a temporary working exterior and a monitoring device for all our activities as incarnated spiritual beings in human forms!

For our better understanding of the above we need to come to know that everything out of the Creator takes on form. In like manner everything that comes out of us also takes on form since we came out of Him! —

God's All -Holy Will which He bellowed into the void immediately manifested in form as His *"Holy Spirit"* Who wields all His creative forces. He is God's embodied *executive* form! This is again revealed in the book. With His creative ability, this embodied Holy Will of the Almighty God, effected all known manifestations of all that now exists in Creation! And in Genesis the Bible says it was God's spirit that walked on the surface of the waters to create all that exists!

This creating was the result of His letting there be the instantaneous amalgamation of alike *Life* giving *Love* energy particles from His Father's *Love only* core; which then formed homogeneous species, realm after succeeding realm of existence and spiritual activities, and which continue to evolve and expand up till now!

Being seeds out of the creative power of the Holy Spirit of God therefore, it is of utmost importance that our words, thoughts and deeds have equivalent spiritual creative powers to take forms here on earth and after here too! This makes us gravely responsible for whether the forms they take for us to see, support our efforts in the achievement of that primal goal for our initial incarnation and subsequent many others, or wether they are detrimental to our success in that crucial endeavour!

For instance, can we confirm that what we as human spirits have said, thought and done since the *"Black Life Matters"* event prompted by George Floyd's murder have helped to enhance our spiritual progress in the right direction, which George himself hoped to remind us all about in his *Mission Karmic* death; or have they rather plunge us collectively and more frighteningly, individually, further into spiritual failure and certain annihilation at this "End Time"? If not, then it is absolutely necessary right now, for every single one of us to begin to re-examine our individual stakes in creation's love based scheme of existence, *only* by sharing the Sublime Love with which He made us! When all is told, we will continue to be the self-made sad victims of our own rather preventable negligence, spiritually and physically. Because since the spirit is in the soul that wears the physical body on earth for visibility and other practical reasons, it manifests symbolic physical malfunctions of one type or another (*illnesses*) that hinder its joyful loving activities visibly on its physically defaulting cloak!

This happens as a result of the misguidance of our *heads* rather than our *hearts*, in discharging our duties as loving human spirits, which leads to making wrong choices and decisions in nearly everything. Derek Chauvin certainly made the wrong decision which took George Floyd's life!

Acts of that nature of which they are many around us and which nature as part of us does not permit, go to amplify the threat we face in her reactions of more damaging but cautioning catastrophic events of the past and present.

These are glaring indications that we can only succeed in maturing in the expected spiritual sense by doing things and living lives strictly based on consistent maintenance of spiritual values with emphasise on relentless loving and caring for one another in every respect and aspect of our mutual spiritual developmental journey on this planet, for which we are all naturally and adequately equipped!

We therefore have no excuse! God loves all of us equally! Not doing as He wills us to do therefore holds us in-escape ably accountable before Him, Who is not only our Creator but Who's essence is only Love and Who requires us to *strictly* adhere to the requirements of His All- Holy Will for our continued existence in the world which He created for us with infinite Love!

Our having been distracted for a long time now and before down the ages from achieving this goal all over the world, is precipitated by the deterring deviant forces of our notorious self- indulgent predisposition among other things to *lusts* for transient power, vanity, self- centred-ness, racism, prejudice superiority complexes and their attendant baggages of discrimination, oppression and exploitation, the acquisition of material wealth, etc., etc.! By all intent and purposes, this has created the demon with seven heads which among other things, has bred humanity's accumulated repercussive visitation of sundry disasters from time to time, now quite expectedly crowned by the vicissitude of the Corona Virus *pandemic*, in the midst of which, all the above material based distracting egotistic concerns have become of little or no import!

This is evidenced by the threatening *collapse* of our current economy, the abandonment of all our pleasurable pastimes and hunts, our forced confinements, deprivations of our cherished common material conveniences, enjoyment of business and pleasure cruises and flights, the merry go lucky sports of the world's *materialists*, even the prioritised pursuit of education, especially in our image making schools and higher institutions of learning etc., etc. All these have made humanity fall back on the survival ill behaviour of self- centredness, symptomatic of a humanity *blindly* against itself simply by failing to *unconditionally* share their Love with one another !

It is this spiritual malpractice of lovelessness which have unavoidably led to the unleashing of the event that brought George Floyd into the cosmic scene of *significant* spiritual magnitude in its impact! It constitutes an event which clearly indicates, in fact *demands* that we and the powers that be in all the nations of the world must now finally *open* our inner eyes and hearts to *reassess* our future roles as living conscientious members of the human race, who should be seeking to attain the same spiritual goal for which we all incarnated on earth to accomplish!

To do this requires the conscientious readjustment of our procedures in the management of the spiritual powers and abilities bestowed upon all of us for it by our Creator.

These powers and abilities distinctly bear only upbuilding and spiritually uplifting fruits, harvested from our words, our thoughts and deeds; which should be in consonance with the Ten Commandments of the Judaic derived religion, and exists in other forms in other world religions with doctrinal variations!

These unavoidable universal *spiritual imperatives* will however remain unattainable, if we continue living lives that only have selfish material values; in which case we will definitely face the reality of unavoidable destruction as clearly prophesied in the Revelations! The dreadful scenarios have already began to play out in the escalation of ominous manmade and natural global disasters that daily stare us all in the face, to challenge and alert us!

Events like that of the insensitivity of the brutal murderers of George Floyd, in the playing out of his Mission karma, was therefore auspiciously meant to shock humanity back to their senses and ultimately draw our attention back to striving to fulfil that most important reason for being alive in this world, which is to attain *complete* spiritual maturity through the practice of *unconditional sublime Love* as willed by our Maker!

Why Then George Floyd

Many times before, humanity in separate parts of our world, had faced repercussive scourges the like of which we are now having to grapple with. This type of fall-out from our spiritual delinquencies is now indisputably occurring globally, demanding everyone's attention more than ever before! We would do best therefore to encourage each other to open our inner spiritual eyes and see what is *really* afoot. This is necessary because, we are all spirits first and foremost as repeatedly stated before, sojourning here on earth our *"spiritual school"* for practicing all the ramifications of the attributes of Love with which we are all graciously endowed by God the Father Who is Love, and which is the only power and means for success in our existence in His Creation!

To have lived by the power of His sublime Love would have automatically made our world a *replica* of our spiritual home in heaven. That's the meaning of the invocation of the part of the Lord's Prayer that enjoins us to say the following: *"Thy Kingdom come, Thy will be done on earth as it is in heaven"*! This was not a metaphor but an injunction to be fulfilled by mankind themselves! We are the ones to make this happen while we are here, not God because His abode is not here as we are all aware. But He has given us all the requisite spiritual and material resources with which to do so, and topped it up with the spiritual guiding principles for our success, in His Ten Commandments and the three other major natural laws of Creation enunciated in the book mentioned earlier. But unfortunately, as the global events of the past and present day bear witness, we as humanity have not lived up to God's expectations, but failed to carry out our own share of making our world a replica of heaven; from not living by the rules, as stipulated in the said commandments! Rather we have turned our world into a spiritually mutated jungle of abominable emblems of darkness, represented by such as contributed to the event that led to George Floyd's cruel death!

This event stands out as an eye-opener to humanity's *deplorable* spiritual plight at this point in time!

A serious look everywhere, at the daily endeavours of all the races of mankind, be it in the cities or the jungles of the remotest corners of the world will confirm this, and reveal the consequent daily ominous indications of the "*escalation*" of *repercussive natural and manmade catastrophes* that will continue to escalate and finally overwhelm us, whose activities in creation emit *spiritual* energy radiations that have become incompatible with the energy of Love with which *all nature* operates as willed by our Creator! This is sure to happen if we fail to act in the meantime in our own favour, by doing all in our *spiritual* and material power to bring about the prevention of more atrocities of any nature in our world- *the should be replicated spiritual kingdom of God on earth!*

We can accomplish this physically and spiritually only by expressing the *sublime Love* we all bear to one another without exceptions and under all circumstances and in all locations; irrespective of our colour, our creed, our political views and philosophies, our education or lack of it! It also means that we should do our best to *desist* from encouraging each other to fall back into our usual euphoric *self- complacency* after every disaster; devoting all our efforts in restoring our material losses in exclusion of any spiritual orientations of all our daily proceedings henceforth! This spiritual debilitating habit is unfortunately buttressed by our misconceived "*Faith*," in putting everything in the hands of the supposedly "*doting*" God of any religion, in the belief that He, the deity of one designation or another, will *indulge* us and at that, arbitrarily, in the misconstrued conception of His/ Her omnipotent benevolence! He/ She will right all our wrongs and *provide* for us! This attitude only lols us to the spiritual sleep of death in the *ensued self-complacency!*

We should rather now take up the responsibility of critically examining our individual as well as our collective spiritual contributions at this point in time, to the proliferation of all that is evil in our society and the world at large; and very much against the adamantine will of God! That is one of the lessons of the event that took place at George Floyd's murder.— Critical *self examination* is demanded from us, to see how we may have contributed to it in however small way! This is because *the book of the spiritual truth of existence said that not a speck of dust will be remitted to any defaulting spirit being in the end!*…

A brief survey of our life preoccupations and inner conflicts, might enable us get the hint of what and how we may have unwittingly comprised ourselves. For instance, many of us have had and still have many *unanswered* question about many *inexplicable and unfavourable* events in our lives during which our reactions have been spiritually and socially questionable to say the least! These events may have been related to our past or ongoing relationships with our fellowmen, beginning with our spouses, or co-workers or even our children, or our brothers and sisters in Faith.

Our health and material conditions top the list of the motivations for the negative thoughts, words or actions which may have compromised our spirits! We may also have had or still have troubling thoughts about the future of not only ourselves but of the whole of mankind, hampered by our status, or our race and other biases that impair our clear judgements of events in their spiritual context: coming from the inexplicable things that may have happened to us and is also happening to people in different parts of the world; burying our misgivings in our acquired misguiding religious doctrines and philosophies! Those without, mostly looking to science or the social media for some form of directions or simply *throwing up their hands*, to amble through life *spiritually* blind and deaf! And yet we are spirits on a special mission on earth! In general, these attitudes have resulted in our day to day insecurity and fear of what might go wrong at any time! And when it does, we turn around and puzzle about how it could have possibly happened despite our professed *Faiths*, our education, our wealth or scientific and technological know hows, our enviable social status, or our down-trodden one: *totally* oblivious of our ongoing debilitating, *spiritually inhibiting* vain and underlying destructive *self-complacent* attitudes; brought about by our palliative dependency on money and technology above all, buttressed by our confessed *blind faith* rather than by proven *compliance to the adamantine* Will of God as enunciated in the Ten Commandments of the Christian Faith and expressed differently in other religious exegesis!

God's All-Holy Will which operates through the immutable aforementioned three primordial laws of creation, one of which is the law of "Reciprocal Action"- What you sow you must reap. (What goes around comes around), stipulates that: If we want to have peace in our world, we must act peaceably. If we want to have Sublime Love in our world, we must cultivate *sublime unconditional loving!* If we want tolerance, the same, if racial and social equity; the same is expected of us all, in whatever office or position we hold in our various communities! Not complying to the demands and guidance of these laws *compromises* our spiritual integrity and leads to our failure as children of God!

And the delusion of a secured redemption by a great percentage of mankind from the consequences of ignoring one of the very important three guiding principles of the adamantine Natural Laws of God cited above, in the belief of the *shedding* the blood of Jesus Christ; has created the spiritual deadening attitude of complacent *superiority of "self"* over and above that of the Creator Himself! Who is then paid hypocritical lip services in honour and sham worship, with edifices of His ludicrous *subservient* sacrifice to *none other than Himself,* Who strangely enough is at the same time both the giver and the recipient of the said *propitiatory* sacrifice!

While we the offenders in our pitiful egocentric selves, not only award ourselves clemency *but* claim we are in the position to command God's responses and services at any given time! That our supreme Creator is at our beck and call, to perform wonders for our *self glorification* and pleasure! All in the twisted notion of a supine Love which *does not exist!* Because God in His unswerving, unyielding perfection of essence and omniscience, operates with the unbiased severity of His Sublime Love at all times; giving rise to the manner of the operation of all His Laws which cannot be changed! Hence *"What one sows one must reap"!* And since God did nothing wrong to anyone, why would He reap the killing of Himself, through His own Son, to appease Himself !!!

Where is God's perfection in this *illogical* juxtaposition of intensions? Where the sanctity and purity of all His actions! And why would one of His Natural Laws of existence be that of a reciprocal nature designated as the *Law of Reciprocal Action,* which is that of sowing and reaping what is sown? Is

God deceiving us or playing with us, letting us endure all unnecessary repercussive hardships, when after all He had already taken all the responsibilities of their consequences by His apparent suicide through His son!

Despite the incongruity of the above spiritual anomaly, the Church leaders all over the world, revel with their ever sensational money oriented congregations, in their *magical* ability to *induce* responses from their *doting* deity! Visit any of the teaming money raking churches that now swam the globe and see for yourself !

We cannot deny that, by all our global money oriented preoccupations, driven by our overdeveloped intellect, we have unwittingly allowed *the audacious encroachment on all the prerogatives of the Creator of all that is*, which is a blatant violation of the guiding humble natural principles of life founded only on *spirituality based on Divine Truth!* This has led us to doing things that are not spiritually beneficial nor even socially acceptable to one anther, let alone to our Creator!

Like the killing of anyone, let alone His Son; and in the case at hand- the gruesome event of George Floyd's suffocation!

In our continued spiritual *sleep of death*, we have hardly ever paid attention to that stated governing law of Reciprocal Action- *What you sow you must reap,* which makes the crucifixion of Jesus Christ, *Who did no wrong* and Who taught us the law, an act of defiance to God; by which we incurred the most severe and tale-telling spiritual *corrective repercussions*, playing out karmically with mankind as we speak, in different locations all over the world: Such as can be detected in the known and hidden cases of "*stigmata*"and other related Divine karmaic manifestations on guilty individuals, and not of any blessings as most people *deludedly* think! Geopolitical and ecological happenings of disastrous natures are included!

Now comes the dastardly murder of George Floyd which fades to insignificance in comparison with that of the *crucifixion* of our Lord Jesus Christ! However, it is revealed that in the *universally unbiased* operation of God's immutable *Law of Reciprocal Action*, just as those individuals who were directly and physically involved in one way or another in the crucifixion of our Lord Jesus on the cross, have come back with *bleeding* palms *or bleeding crowns of their heads* from the crown of thorns they made Him wear, the perpetrators of the suffocation of George Floyd are sure to have earned themselves some karmaic *stigma* in their next incarnation! These happenings go to explain the otherwise inexplicable anomalies of children being born with one disability or another as symbolic results of what they did in their past lives!

Everyone's spiritual *safe net* for a fulfilled life free of bad karma then is for us all to always bear in mind that: The consequences of our wrong past, which we are to face and endeavour to eradicate in our repeated incarnations, notably that of cruelty, human rights abuse, injustice, racism, greed, immorality, prejudice and all the other ills of humanity; *do not escape their deserved repercussions to the perpetrators*, individually and globally, in the irrevocable justice of the *Law of Reciprocal Action!*

It is gratifying to know that its effects which are graver and more spiritually precise and decisive, are *lovingly* aimed at nothing but taming and eradicating all the many deviant acts of humanity; and are therefore indispensable for achieving ultimate success in our struggle for spiritual consciousness and maturity which is the only purpose for our existence!

It is all out of God's Love for all His children, that with the execution of His perfect Laws, He *tames* and *reconstructs!*

They do these by taking into account all the acts of the persecuted and the persecutors over many encounters in many designated shared earth lives. This is because

"*One*" earth life is logistically not enough for the untangling of all the karmic threads that had been spun round both parties in any of their shared lifetimes! That is why we reincarnate. Preachers however take the issue of the "*One*" biblical earth life after which there comes judgement *too literally*. The essence of the Bible being one that only construes events in their *spiritual* context, generally depicts life as it is meant to be for a human spirit, which in this case is *"one" everlasting life*. Therefore, in the Divine scheme of existence, the spirit cosmically lives only "*one life*" which is *one extended life* that lasts through *eternity*! But due to the misguidance of the overdeveloped human intellect, the spirit does the living *intermittently*. However, this periodic truncation applies only to the mortal human body which harbours the intellect in the earthly frontal brain, and not to the *spirit which doesn't ever die!* Our physical bodies are therefore shed in death many more times than the said one life, to afford the bungling human spirit enough time necessary for its accomplishment of the *required* spiritual improvements, meant to lead to the attainment of its *spiritual maturity* in the *"Spiritual School of Love"* of the Earth!

So we do return to the earth school again and again until we qualify to serve our Creator in His ever expanding universes in one *up-building* capacity or another! That is the unalterable Divine intention for creating the world and putting us in it in the first place! This earth is indeed only our *"Spiritual School"*! Viewed in this light, we can see how we human spirits learnt and emulated the normal workings of the universe in our own establishment of schools and other places of learning, where we are required to *repeat* our courses in oder to attain the required qualifications for our different inputs in the society.—

That the societies of the world have not spiritually benefitted from all our now mutated materially oriented schooling, all these eons of years, is clearly evident in the *conflicts* that take place in all human affairs today, devoid of all spiritual considerations whatsoever, especially, in the relationship and governance of the people at large; which glaringly lacks the exercise of the spiritual attributes of the Love of God! Evident in most governors, presidents, prime ministers, kings and queens and all their governed rich and poor, peasants and lords, beggars and vagabonds, thieves and other strata and members of the human race, in short in all present day humanity! There is conflict everywhere, because we lack *spirituality* even though we may consider ourselves *religious*! The two are not the same. Spirituality is *natural* while religiosity is a man-made *acquisition* of a Faith!

Intuitively however, the natural *spiritually endowed Sublime Love* from God in all of us including George Floyd, who must have experienced the effect of our failure to love one another the way we should in many life times as we all have, and had *learnt* many lessons thereby; that living and mostly ignored *intuition* in *all* human spirits, must have *encouraged* him to undertake the "*Mission Karma*" of shocking humanity back to recognising their wrong doing: Namely, in *not implementing* that *imperative* spiritual requirement of the conscious expression of *unconditional sublime love* to one another at all times; which is the only way to attain *that* common goal of *spiritual maturity* in the earth school! In other words, George Floyd reincarnated this time on the special mission, out of his spiritual desire to help us all reawaken the *sublime love* lying dormant in us, ever waiting to be employed in doing that which all human spirits should have been lovingly doing to one another since the world began.

Failing to do so as Derek and his mates did, and as millions of humanity do, especially at this "*End Time*", makes what George Floyd did in his mission, most heroic and worthy of praise! That the world reacted as he must have expected, by condemning the murderous act, means that he succeeded in that mission of waking the world up from their sleep of *spiritual death*; not withstanding some insignificant dissenting voices of those still in their *spiritual coma of complacency!*

The prophesied "*End Time*" of judgement is going to be brought about by the fact that all efforts at the reformation and realignment of humanity's faulty ways of life to accord with the *immutable* All-Holy Will of God over millions of years of our spiritual evolution *have failed!* Therefore we should not be surprised to be witnessing to our dismay, all the ongoing deluge and upsurge of avalanches of personal as well as world wide devastations of catastrophic proportions ever to have taken place in recorded human history!

These are happening as the *fruits* of our endemically misdirected human pursuits, which are focused primarily on all that is disproportionally *material!* These upset the maintenance of spiritual *equilibrium*, by jarring the harmony of frequencies in the vibrations and resultant radiations we *regularly* emit into the ether from all our activities for our ethereal wellbeing! With those *destructive* types of radiations we have been emitting these eons of years, our immediate etheric surroundings are leaden with spiritually irritating elements that must now be flung back to their originators in symbolic experiential codes in the just Law of Reciprocal Action!

That is why we should each celebrate George Floyd for his *sacrifice* in spiritually choosing to serve his fellowmen the way he did, to remind us of who we truly are and what we should *not* be doing here on earth by disobeying God's all Holy Will; *which is to love one another unconditionally!* We should always also remember that the Lord Jesus Christ said, He would not heed those who ceaselessly call His name, but only *those who do His Father's Will* which primarily concerns *loving and serving others as we love and serve ourselves!* If the police officers loved George as they do themselves, they would not have stood by and allow him to be suffocate to death; because they too would not want that to be their own fates! Besides, Derek Chauvin would not have knelt on his neck, ignoring the poor man's pleas to be allowed to breath; but unfeelingly stifling George's precious life out of him!

As things are, you and I will therefore not admit that we have *not* been emulating our Lord Jesus Christ in His steadfastness of purpose and compliance to the laws of His Father. Things have therefore gone from bad to worse and now without a doubt, dangerously out of control!

The aforementioned laws of Creation namely:(1) the law of Reciprocal Action (2) The Law of Attraction of Homogeneous Species and (3) The law of Gravity, all which *determine* our overall spiritual and material fates are automatically called into action by the manner in which we apply our inherent abilities doing *anything* whatsoever every moment of our lives; as explained in the special knowledge given to mankind at this time. The misuse or abuse of our spiritually endowed abilities in *all capacities of life* therefore is tantamount to us cutting off our noses to spite our own faces! Because doing so *undermines all possibilities of real* success in life as far as the spirit is concerned, for we will be in perpetual conflict with the modus operandi of the *spiritual beings* that we are, who are *unequivocally* under God's control and rulership, through the tutelage of His three Laws, since He is the one Who made us to operate by those laws and gave us the life we have!

Once again, not taking serious cautions of these governing Primordial Laws of Creation, is the cause of our continued individual as well as all our global problems manifesting in many different forms, especially in that of our continued *loveless acts;* clearly demonstrated at the murderous scene of George Floyd! Nevertheless, as the laws are called into action by our activities, such acts have already triggered off their just operation with their attendant pleasant or most likely unpleasant fruits for the perpetrators of the said act!

Having experienced the unpleasant fallouts of the *breached* primordial laws in our past incarnations in many different ways, it is expected that before our present incarnations we would have planned to *alter* our incurred unfavourable conditions by *altering* our individual perspectives on life this time, to attune to *doing only what is good* in the will of God; through our form-taking words, thoughts and actions, and that we would always be mindful of those most valuable primordial Just and Loving Laws of Creation which strictly operate in the *All-Holy Will of our Creator*! Failing to do so triggers off continuous unfavourable requisite *disharmony* in our communities; which continue to induce disasterous occurrences like George Floyd's murder and hosts of others in our societies, all of which cosmically go to trigger off the natural catastrophes we experience; in the due *reaction* of Creation's love based *rectifying mechanism* of the said laws in the affairs of man! Meaning that we will continue to suffer all the endemic atrocities, coupled with their escalating natural and man-made disasters that will certainly lead to our annihilation at this End Time.

George Floyd spiritually volunteered to help us *forestall* the *pending* unleashing of our incurred grave and devastating karma with his special "*Mission Karmic*" death. The least we can do is to individually *wake up* from our *complacency* and de-emphasise our reliance on the *defying earth- bound* intellect, which has *suppressed* our spirits and forced us to continue to ignore and *defy* God's Will, which jeopardises our chances of our eternal survival! No one can either physically nor spiritually survive without doing *God's Will, especially at this "End Time!"* As spirits we are meant to live for eternity under well defined spiritual conditions which are immutable. It is in our best interest therefore to strictly and consistently observe those conditions!

The Candle In The Dark

The evolutionary science refers to the physical *long process* of the appearance of man on earth, which is retroactively the process by which God *divinely* allowed a portion of His emitted spirit sparks to take forms as *spirit seed-grains*, which for their development, were granted the desire to traverse the embryonic arena of Creation, from their original home, in the realm of spiritual substantiality, referred to as *paradise*: to undergoing equally prolonged developments, step by step, from one ethereal realm to another; to finally enter the ready developed animal body in the earthly physical realm as revealed in the aforementioned spiritual book. The entering occurred by *radiation* at a given time, as the final step towards adorning the cloak of the *human* body for the completion of the last phase of their spiritual development!

This spiritual process was executed by His Holy Will - "*The Holy Spirit*" - God's "*executive*" *personality*, Who had created everything in the aforementioned Fiat:" *Let there be light*". He did it by first *raising the ready* evolved animal to its feet, with the *spiritual self-willing ability* of the spiritually evolving man, that then displaced the *instinctive group-drive* of the *animal soul!*

This radiation process is reminiscent to some degree, of the entrance of the embodiment of *Divinity* through *Divine* radiation into the foetus in Mary's womb at the right time, *transforming* it from a mere human spirit's incarnation to a Divine incarnation!

In the further process of evolution, the *incarnated* young spirit in the animal body, was meant to mature into a viable conscious human spirit in form and behaviour, in a progressive ennoblement of the *crude characteristics* and inclinations of the original animal; by operating with the power of his now *intuitive spiritual* abilities, rather than those of his former *instinctive* mere animal *soul* abilities.

It is sad to observe however, that some large proportion of humanity still maintain to some degree, our *former* coarse animal behaviours till date! This is coming from our failure to strictly adhere to the omnipresent guidance of God, through our *intuition*, which leads *only* to the execution of *all that is good* : a distinctive *life* preserving endowment, inherent in all human spirits! Those are our true birth rights! While a *regression* into our original animal instinctive behaviours, make us do things to each other, like what was done to George Floyd and other members of the world society during wars and all forms of combats and various manners of discordant relationships!

This account of the coming into existence of the spiritual man, technically proves that the *after-the-fact* investigations and dicoveries of the evolutionists, about creation at only the physical level; caught up only with the physical changes that took place in the appearance of the *physical* man on earth and not with the spiritual creationists knowledge of "*Divine initiative,*" in the origination of man! The discrepancy lies in the fact that science is distinctly a product of the *intellect* which is unfortunately only earth-bound, and *totally incapable* of diciphering anything spiritual! So, at the *physical* level which is the field of operation of the intellect, the evolutionists were able to catch up only with the physical changes that took place in the appearance of the *physical* man on earth!

Not being only physical beings, but spirits cloaked with perishable physical bodies, how then is it possible to expect that we can function with continued *disregard* of the *Will* of the Divine *initiator*, which is intricately woven into the strict operation of all that was manifested in this very unique process? Disregarding the requirements of God's all holy and adamantine Will, as to how to function in the *spiritually and* physically evolving world, as we continue to do up till now, has definitely put us all in conceivable danger!

And we are all now witnessing the *fallouts* from this hubris everyday in our homes, our streets, and in all of our communities round the globe! Therefore reincarnation for atonement and reform will continue even within the short time left for our judgement, as we trudge along *burdened* with requisite consequences for our intransigences which *cannot* be swept under any pretentious religious, political, social or cultural carpets, past or present: Because God's All-Holy Will *cannot continue to be subjugated*!

The havoc our consistent abuses and unbridled dependency on the *dictates* of our *overdeveloped* intellect, rather than on our spiritually backed intuition, has reduced us to *revellers* in what is spiritually grotesque and unexpected of true human beings! Turned us into totally materially oriented zombies, *irresponsive* to the *promptings* of the small voice of the spirit within us, and made us remain *bound* to the commands of our frontal brain; which directs us to pursue all what is only *temporal*! This definitely militates against the necessary cultivation of what is of *the greatest* importance to our more *immortal* spirits; in its obstruction of our struggle to truly achieve that spiritual goal we came to do here !

As things are, it seems we prefer to be reincarnating over and over again, to suffer all forms of well deserved repercussions; which may manifest in so many different ways, including for example, our being subjected to deprivations, because we deprived our fellow spirits in former lives! Or may be oppressed, abused, scandalised, tortured, even murdered! Or suffer other forms of atrocities for the same reason! All which we are experiencing now in one form or another, everywhere; is because *we must reap what we have sown* back here on earth or in the beyond, for our own spiritual reformation and redemption. Any state in which we may consequently find ourselves in any incarnation, affords us the necessary opportunity to *atone* for those past wrong deeds and effect a spiritually acceptable noble change in the new life! So we need to make good use of all our sore and unfavourable karmaic conditions and experiences, without blaming anyone else but ourselves at any given time!

There are a sundry variations in the types of reincarnation, which brings George Floyd into a scene of momentous cosmic proportion! That is the main reason why this work - "Why George Floyd" is delving into the implications of his death!

On the surface, we appear to be disassociated with the reason for his manner of death. But in *spiritual* reality, we *are all very much involved!* How is that? One may ask. We forget that our body for which we care so much, is only a *physical* tool which came from the dirt of the earth and returns there at death, prompting the saying "Dust to dust and ash to ash". We do this in *total negligence* of our *immortal* spirit, the more important partner of our *dual* entity, which we leave marooned in the twilight zone of the beyond! This entity within us is vibrationally and subliminally *connected* to all others in the world, through that law of attraction of *homogeneous species* - in thoughts, words and deeds! We therefore visibly and *invisibly* affect each other's actions, via the radiations of our words, thoughts and our deeds; encouraging each other or discouraging each other, inciting or calming each other; uplifting or inspiring each other to do good or bad: to do just anything at all, because we are all of the human species and are therefore spiritually connected and never really operate alone! It literally means that whatever we want to do, our fellowmen indeed are our *coworkers* of spiritual and material wonders, or *accomplices* in committing heinous crimes against humanity, *if we* are so inclined! That which drove George Floyd to take up the supposed spiritual responsibility of going through the trauma of a Mission "*Karmic*" death: is therefore prompted by our collective failures to live exemplary lives now and in many lives before; of expressing the ever *indispensable* unconditional sublime Love to each other, as was evidently demonstrated by his murderers!

As a warning that this exemplary act of *unconditional Love* of a voluntary Mission Karmic death, to be given by George, was again not going to be reciprocally shown to him and people like him by insensitive selfish humanity, consistently courting its own destruction; (by revelling in the perpetration of acts of disobedience to the Will of God) is spiritually: what might have motivated George Floyd to take on the aforesaid grave responsibility, meant to help us mitigate the repercussion of total destruction of our spirits which is now looming over us at this "End Time"!

Our Suicidal Lifestyle

How can we *change*, to save ourself from the above, resulting from the automatic *adverse* reactions of the natural laws of creation, which *we* set in motion by our spiritual noncompliant actions; the repercussive manifestations of which we then *wrongly* term the" *Wrath*" of God! Such known devastating manifestations of global significance include the flood in Noah's day, the Red Sea event against Egypt, the recent tsunamis and many plagues of history of which the pandemic of today's world are but a few.

Our only hope of effecting any changes is for us to first and foremost *remember* that we are *spirits* who our Father in heaven granted the wish, as revealed in the one of a kind spiritual work for all mankind at this time and indeed for all times, which *categorically* states that we were *spirit* grains who evolved into spirit germs with free wills, who were granted the wish to come down to earth to develop our spiritual personalities to the fullest, and through that, ennoble ourselves and our environments! We are then supposed to do it by expressing all the loving attributes that He, the Creator endowed us! The over all intension being that in the process of doing this, we would fully mature as spirits and become the likenesses of His Image! Nothing more and nothing less!...

But then we arrived here and within a short period of cosmic time, allowed ourselves to be distracted by all that is material, forgetting our original purpose as *spirits*, who are only wearing the physical material flesh as a tool for attaining that goal on the material physical world, which we are also expected to transform into a beautiful, pure and happy place for mankind of all colours and creed!

This negligent and frivolous obsessive greedy life of doing anything it may take for the insatiable acquisition of material wealth, constitute the main reasons the world is in such a mess in all aspects of life and therefore, not resembling the home above which we were meant to replicate!

The insensitive attitudes of most of the materially affluent human spirits towards the exploited and neglected majority of mankind, was amply metaphorically portrayed in a post on facebook by someone which I shared. In that post, an absolutely pathetic, shrivelled, abandoned, hungry, terrified, shivering and emaciated dog was lurking in a desolate corner of a street, looking very unfriendly and dangerous! Many avoided him as they passed by or perhaps were even scared of him and dared not do anything to help him! Then the animal rescuers came along and with patience and humane tender care, calmed him down and gained his trust with their Love! The scene was so heart rending and reminiscent of our human life circumstances that I could not hold back hot tears streaming down my face!

I shed the tears watching the happening, comparing it to the prevalent outbursts of intimidations, physical, political and religious violence and terror everywhere in our societies today! Seeing the playing out of the same outrageous predicament of the deprived and uninformed citizens of all nations even as we speak!

Wishing we can rescue humanity from the infliction of this magnitude that has reduced most of humanity to wimps or violent brutes! The dog's abandonment had made it react with fear and violence, brought about by its insecurity, distrust and need. But through the kindness, patient understanding and tender caring considerations of the rescuers, the dog felt "*loved*" again and with trust, *reciprocated* with his Love!

So it is with human beings, because that is what love does any time and in any place! We are spiritual beings that can *only function properly* when we are loved and do not ourselves *fail* to treat others with Love! George Floyd emotionally and materially represented many who are like that dog, in a society that has broken them and *silenced* them with *unjust* systems, cruelty and greed: a society that has become insensitive to people who have been abandoned by a selective social and political system that has declared them *unworthy* and certainly *undeserving* of any help, clemency nor Love, let alone to be regarded as fellow human beings! He represented the down trodden and *so called* inferior race; as determined by the acclaimed privileged branch of the human race *which does not exist* in God's Creation; but only in man's deluded and bigoted opinion of his intellectualised, narrow minded and physically oriented world view!

He lay there, *pleading* for the return of humanity to their original Loving, sensitive and responsive selves, to their *considerations* of other's needs to exist and share God's abundance of grace and Love! He lay there, *begging* for his *life*, in the hands of another fellow human spirit, who had certainly forgotten his life's purpose! He lay there, that the world may recognise the *condemnable* result of the continued *deprivation* of this sublime indispensable essence of *Love* in all of us and in all that exists!

The whole world did recognise and *rebelled* in *condemnation* of Derek Chauvin's murderous act, which violated the *supreme* power of unrestricted universal sublime Love!—

That's why the past and present agitations,
That's why the threatening insurrections,
The hustling and rumbling,
The wagging of tongues,
And the throwing of stones!
The confusion and consternation;
The apprehension of the inevitable....-
But providence has taken an emergency step
In a monumental "George Floyd" counter event -
Putting darkness under house arrest;
So mankind can cat-scan itself
And effect the necessary damage control-
And save all humanity at this "End Time"
From total annihilation!

More Than Meets The Eye

We were given all we need for our successful existence in the material world, through the control and exercise of our spiritual back brain known as the *cerebellum*. But the over-cultivation of the intellect in our frontal brain known as the *cerebrum*, which does not understand spirituality, but excels in all things of its limited material nature, as a means for our manipulating and solving "only *earthly*" challenges: has *overshadowed* the input of our spiritual brain! This aberration has duly resulted in all the chaotic happenings in our world!

The back brain is to inform and *direct* the intellectual brain, not the other way around!

This pervading anomaly originated at the time of the "Fall of man", when man succumbed to the over- riding of the spiritual intuitive ability of his back brain by the intellectual rationalisations of his frontal brain, in the temptation of Lucifer in the garden of Eden: a symbolic spiritual plane in the evolutionary journey of man, as he descended from paradise to earth, and not here on earth as people mistake it to be! Again this is revealed in the afore-mentioned one of a kind book- *In The Light of Truth- The Grail Message* by Add-ru-shin. It is one of the many revelations from The Light for the clarifications of some commonly misconstrued religious concepts and much of the spiritual chronicles in the Bible; which the author found necessary to do at this "Cosmic Turning Point" known as the "End Time" for our correct understanding of all spiritual events and processes in the world, once and for all!!

With that understanding we can then easily discern the causes and meanings of all that transpires in the cosmos, which will prevent us from destroying our chances for lasting survival in a constantly challenging world, thereby averting many otherwise would be catastrophic repercussions! We would certainly avoid developing into living *self-centred* and insensitive lives, where only materially successful groups of individuals or nations have any say in the affairs of man, just as it is now. A world where such alone share the world's cakes among themselves! Where the so called underdogs are *trampled underfoot and gagged* and their human rights *even to live*, are denied by governing bodies of elites!

To them it is, that George Floyd and anyone else who feels the pressure of the mounting weight of cold indifference, born out of the degree of lovelessness in our world; are appealing for allowance to "*breath*" the air of Life Giving Unconditional Love now before it is too late!

For the achievement of this, the Omniscient Creator preemptively gave us all what it will take for us to succeed at all times right from birth! He endowed us with:-

The gift of the five senses
For mastering all life's phases
Gaining the spiritual posture,
For His Will cannot be opposed!
He gave us noses
To breath for our lives -
Yet George was this denied!
He gave us two eyes
To see what pleases,

Crowns of the head
To house our discerning brains,
Evaluating all events
With appropriate concern.
God gave us two arms
For offering helping hands.
Our mouths and lip
For uttering loving words

With calm and charm!

Gave us our brave hearts,
To beat with Love and not with lust
Nor to plot to hurt,
Gave us our two lungs,
To nurse the air they pump.
Gave us our tongues-
To speak the truth with all resolve !
Gave each a pair of ears
To hear all with good cheer.

A pair of hands to work the land
To fill our barns.
Gave each two strong feet,
To walk and explore the fields.
Gave us the gift of Love
To give to the world -
No matter the case,
No matter the place,
No matter the shape or race!

In his "spiritual" developmental reincarnations, as we all have been doing, George Floyd must have certainly experienced much of the inappropriate nor spiritually supportive acts, born from the inhibitions of the usurping intellect in which we have all been willingly indulging, and which are totally not only at variance but are *grossly in defiance* of the Will of God! This has without a doubt driven mankind to the development of systems that have encouraged the domination of one group of human spirits over others, and generated all the atrocities committed as a result; so much so that this time around as said, George decided to do something spiritually significant to arrest the seemingly endless loveless trend! What he chose to do, which is consonant with the spirit of Love, was something selfless and solicitude. He did it in order to help bring about the much needed spiritual reorientation of all humanity in all spheres of life!

George is however not alone in spiritual engagements. You and I are subliminally aware of humanity's failures in the cosmic order of things. You and I have therefore reincarnated incalculable number of times, just to put things right; but unfortunately, we continue to allow ourselves to be distracted by all that are spiritually *irrelevant* and destructive! We continue to turn away from anything that will remotely remind us of our *spiritual responsibilities* and refocus us on facing ourselves by owning to our faults. We look for excuses in externals. We complain about the weather and the economy not favouring us and other things to that effect. We hide under the cover of our misfortunes which we have brought upon ourselves by the way, and blame our fates or God, making us lose faith in Him and all He stands for! Making us abandon the *prompting of our consciences*, leading to our ignoring the pursuit of our original purpose in life, of attaining spiritual maturity; which is far removed from the loveless and obsessive insensitive and materialistic pursuits which has preoccupied us in its place, from one century to another, one epoch to another, one millennium to yet another!...

Our continued obstinate noncompliant attitude in this spiritual matter has born the bitter fruit which we must all now consume!

Everything we now do is practically devoid of any spiritual stimulus, and so has only led to the sufferings of wars, famines, economic malaise of various kinds, political and religious upheavals, terrorisms, insurrections and civil demonstrations here and there; to call attention to all the abuses and atrocities which continue to destroy our chances as spirits, of attaining our true purpose for incarnation! In the agitation, we are supported by nature's increase of *karmic* catastrophes which are falling back on us now more frequently than ever before! And this, in place of the peace and happiness we were meant to reap from our sown seeds of the power of *Unconditional Love* for one another!

You and I should therefore think seriously about the auspicious intervention by George and not treat it with the usual nonchalance, because in truth, we are spirits that live for ever! Spirits who are lovingly permitted to reincarnate to reevaluate themselves after each earth life prior to returning to earth each time; so to know exactly what to redo and improve, or what new upbuilding contributions to make for the achievement of our engrained and inescapable common spiritual goal!

That's why George Floyd is certainly not alone in this endeavour. Reincarnation is the rule of necessity and not an exception for special human spirits. It happens out of the Love of the Creator, as a means of helping us mature in the experiences we go through each time, which we however don't remember that we had pre-planned in the beyond before we reincarnate; only to be again misled, sidetracked or thwarted by prevalent earthly indulgences! Each life on earth is therefore an indispensable opportunity given to us to make a useful upbuilding contribution not only for our individual spiritual development, but also for that of humanity as a whole! That is why George Floyd played the part he did.

Our bodies as said, on the other hand are only the physical cloak in which our spirits physically perform on the *physical* earth, and decay soon after our physical death. Unfortunately, with our self imposed limited understanding of who we are and what we are to be doing here on earth, we have channelled all our talents and energy into only catering for the *cloak* to the sad negligence of the *spirit* that uses it only as a *tool* for making the assigned duty of fulfilling our sublime love based mission on earth easier in the supportive *physical* entity! That's why we are failing to achieve that which we all actually came here for, as very clearly demonstrated by the chaotic and loveless nature of all what is happening in the world today; beginning in more familiar terms with the state of our economies, our politics, our health, our entertainment engagement our morals, etc., and above of all our relationships with one another as individuals or as nations: indicating the obvious fact that we are surely going to fail again in our spiritual development, because of our endemic inability to learn the *spiritual lessons* of past civilisation! We continue to remain complacent and satisfied as things are, imagining that we are okay with only science and technology, which are products of the intellect that lacks any spiritual powers: with its scope of support to the spirit, naturally and *strictly limited to the confines of materiality only!* Why do we continue to do this when as spirits we *should be dependent on what is only spiritually rooted!*

The intellect's sham sensational material products which we enjoy and revel in unfortunately endangers our spiritual progress in more ways than one! Because, by the *natural law of homogeneity*, they invariably end up *binding* us to the material world where as spirits we don't belong! This is demonstrated by some of us who *cling so much* to the *earthly* products of the usurping overdeveloped intellect that their *souls* which are the ethereal *cloaks* of the spirits, refuse to leave their earthly *cloaks* of the body in death and are forced to hang on in agonising prolonged death throes! Some linger around favourite homes, bars, clubs, restaurants, jobs and so on, as *ghosts* for endless periods of time until they are released by exorcism or some other means!

No amount of wealth and power that the intellectual manipulation of the gifts of nature can take us to our home in heaven! Neither can that help us in achieving our stipulated spiritual purpose which is not for all the glory of the material world put together! Just as our Lord Jesus Christ said of Himself— truly, our kingdom *is not of this world!*

The limitation that the intellect exacts from those who overuse its services has been proven even today by a survey made about the percentage of people who believe or not believe in the existence of God. The survey revealed that the *more highly educated* one gets, the *less* one is inclined to believe in God!

For instance it was found that while more than 90% of ordinary members of the world population believe in God, the college educated believers drop to 60%! This drops to 40% among *higher degree* holders and then to 7% among specially qualified members of the academia; then further drops to 1% among the *highest* echelons of science! That certainly tells us all we need to know about the havoc that the overdevelopment of the frontal brain has done and continues to do to us! *Our insistence on doing everything the intellect conceives in its cleverness, rather than what the spirit prompts us to do by our conscience or intuition, is what has precipitated the avalanche of cataclysmic retributive happenings today; to individuals as well as nations, as it did before in history! To continue to ignore all these warning signs and experiences is spiritually suicidal, a show of senseless foolhardiness!*

Because our salvation strictly lies in our observing, learning, improving and pursuing goals that have the utmost spiritual values. Not in our handing over our own assigned responsibilities to the Lord Jesus or some other scapegoats! The provisions for our assured success are woven into the fabrics of all the mechanism of Creation by the Creator just for our own good!!!

Metaphorically speaking, God being the *Landlord* and we the *tenants* in His property, *must live by His rules*; or we would be finally evicted with no where else to go but downwards in the beyond after death: into such conditions that defy any conceivable human possible imagination of how *tenacious reaping what one has sown is*, in conveying culprits to places they themselves had automatically built for themselves with their life's conducts; commonly designated as *hell!* There to stay and learn to readjust their future lives to accord with the Will of the said *Landlord*, or reincarnate to make amends that conform with the benevolent Landlord's rules!

It is worth repeating that it is in our well considered interest to force ourselves to wake up from our *spiritual* slumber, because we are not only *indisputable* spiritual beings, wearing the earthly cloak of the physical human body, in the *indisputable* spiritual quest of our spiritual maturity; but also are meant to achieve this, in the equally *indisputable spiritual* school of material earth and its environs! We therefore cannot keep on shelving our duties to our selves! We owe it to ourselves to do nothing else but spend our whole life focusing all our attention on the pursuit of that spiritual maturity for which our most benevolent and omniscient Divine Creator *prepared* us to achieve in so many ways before our incarnation and manifested in such manners as are enumerated below, testifying that at birth:—

We were all colour blind,
Ego blind,
Looks blind,
Status blind,
Nationality blind,
Culture blind,
Demography blind,
Politics blind.

We're all religion blind,
Race blind,
Caste blind,
Heritage blind,
Rights blind,
Gender blind ,
Possession blind,
Blind - to fame and all it takes,
Blind - to hatred and all it take,
Blind - to envy and all it takes,
Blind - to cruelty and all it takes;
To vanity and all it takes,
To power and all it takes,
To greed and all it takes,
To oppression and all it takes.

Blind to dishonestly and all it takes.
To immorality and all it takes.
To homophobia and all it takes.
To racism and all it takes.
To superiority complexes and all it takes.
To slavery and all it takes.
To terrorism and all it takes.
To fanaticism and all it takes.

We were blind to dogmatism, tribalism,
Demagoguery, nepotism and egotism;
To anything that offends,
Anything that hurts,
Anything that degrades,

Why George Floyd

Anything that indoctrinates:
We were blind to all evil
And all they take!

But from one lifetime to another, all the above are forgotten or suppressed and we become *spiritually encumbered* with the development of unsavoury habits and the acquisition of traditional and cultural values, political and religious doctrinal practices that do not advance us on our *needed spiritual* development! Culminating in the deviations from all the spiritual norms enumerated above, but like everything else, have been duly corrupted, through deviant interactions between one man and another or one nation and another; all which have devolved into the overall *disregard of precious human life!* ....*This* was clearly displayed in the event of George Floyd's dastardly murder!

We have acquiesced to acts like these mainly because we had forgotten how to live with the knowledge of *who we truly are* and what we *should* be doing here on earth, in order to achieve that spiritual only goal! Not as some people imagine they are doing by practices of ill conceived occultism in different forms: including clairvoyance or clairaudience, endless meditations, tarot card-readings and spells casting, etc! But *in doing only what is good* to one another! Here is how the Bringer of the one of a kind spiritual work puts it and I quote:

"The Law of the Almighty God for you is : You are permitted to wander through Creation! Go in such a manner as to cause nor harm to others in pursuit of your personal desires!"

He further repeated and I quote:

"And during this wandering you shall not harm any others who like you are also journeying through Creation…"

Summarising both in His quoting of our Lord Jesus Christ's words : " *Love thy Neighbour as thyself* "! Somewhere else He also repeated what our Lord Jesus Christ had also said in all sublimity and simplicity that all we need to do is to *"Do unto others as you would want done to you!"*

But in modern day blind, deaf and insensitive world, we stumble and primarily walk about like zombies: mindless: of who we may *hurt* in our various physical or emotional collisions; with our minds set only on our material goals, and our eyes glued to our phones and other physical gadgets and objects! Our scientific know how, our manmade faulty laws, social status and all the rest, are crowned by our obsessions with the crave for "*Money*"! All of these comfort but spiritually *numb* us, making us ignore everything, including other human beings who could help us look up and see the predicament of how the potential spiritual heroes that we were to be, are now languishing in death dealing spiritual amnesia; totally that we are all *spiritually* connected and are psychically *affecting* one another positively or negatively!

One of the ways in which we affect each other psychically is in our *behaviours* or *character* which is spiritually determined by our sizes, among other karmic factors. ..! And George Floyd was huge!

What does size have to do with it?

Have you never wondered why we are of so many different heights in the world. Is it perhaps just a random act of nature via nutrition and one's gene? Remember nothing comes from nothing! Everything that manifests in Creation has a spiritual beginning or reason. So why does nature endow some people with shortness even among families where parents and other siblings are tall, and why are there some of medium heights and variations of these?

In the language of what manifests in Creation through which the Creator speaks to us, He demonstrates the stipulated means by which nature enforces the spiritually desired implementations of the laws of Creation. Thus all manner of guidance and help to enable us live our lives with Love has been provided; irrespective of how much we ignore or twist and turn within the considerably long time allotted to us to accomplish this!

Some of these helps range from the most spiritual to the most mundane, down even to the natural elements of nature all around us, including even the behaviours of animals. The more discernible are those of bravery and courage in the lion, agility, alertness and grace in the tiger and cheetah, faithfulness in the dog, perseverance in the goat, nobility and the memory of one's spiritual origin in the elephant, implied grace and upward looking in the giraffe, etc. etc.!

These represent some of the *mirrors* we should usefully hold up to ourselves as we strive to become what is expected of us. Other helps include our places of birth, our families and friends, our stations and situations in life, our karma, our race and so on, as you may very well know already. In fact, simply *everything* that has become manifest, spiritually or *physically*, is meant to be of help to the striving human spirit! We only have to open our inner eyes, and consciously avail ourselves of the offer of their helpful presence!

The most dramatic *personal* and motivating help given to us by our Maker, to enable us in *remembering* to strive to achieve the spiritual only goal for which we incarnated on this earth, is our physical *sizes*! What is the connection? One may ask. The answer is thus: With the mechanism of creation not accommodating lapses of any kind in the perpetual automatic weavings of events; the Creator benevolently established the spiritual guidance of letting us carry the measure and value of our spiritual achievements or lack of it on our personal *statures*. This is meant to remind us of how much we have achieved or still need to achieve from one lifetime to another!

Keeping the picture of people of the stature of George Floyd in our mind's eyes, how then do our different statures help us in this context? It is important to bear in mind that there is no one on earth today who does not have something to redeem before His Creator! The Christian says that *we have all sinned and fallen short of His Grace!* But I believes that much grace yet abounds in that which I am now going to bring to your notice and objective evaluation.

A tall man or woman more often than not *instinctively* desires a partner who is shorter, resulting in both having to always *physically look down* on the one who is lower in height! Could this not be merely a *physical* reaction or interpretation to that which is actually *spiritual?* In our human existence, everything that happens has a spiritual origin and meaning, because everything is spiritual. The inclinations of the two human spirits can then be seen as a *helpful* indication to the fact that, it is more desirable for such individuals to strive to *cultivate* the virtue of *uplifting humility* above all other attributes of Divine Love which may still be weak in them!

In George Floyd it is most predictable that because of his spiritual advancement in experiences of past lives, he had cultivated the practice of *virtuous* existence, which includes that of *humility* in his compliance to the Will of the Creator, which then reciprocally *elevated* him and others like him, through the workings of the Natural Laws of existence, to the height he and they grew to be on earth! Consequently, operating subliminally with the promptings of his many past life's experiences, he was then able to further undertake the *high* Mission Karmic reincarnation of the present time! In passing I like to mention the fact that it is known that earlier in human evolutionary account, more innocent humanity was made up of giants, whose fossils and skeletons have been authenticated by archeologists!

However, since our purpose is to develop all our spiritual qualities *equally*, when there is a weakness in any, it *drags us down spiritually* That's why although some spirits may have variably excelled in most of the expected virtuous qualities, as may truly be the case for those whose former spiritual upward growth is *mirrored* in the physical elevation of their stature, there may yet be some *unsavoury* attitudes left in the characters of this category of human statures!

These may include some *left over* traits of pride, prejudice, presumptuousness, intolerance, heightened sense of self, to name a few. There is also the lingering danger of perhaps harbouring a sense of superiority and condescension towards others, stemming from a previous life of having *material success*, or piety without the practice of all the aspects of the virtues of true Living Love as is expected of everyone of us!

Therefore, in the present life time, the symbolism of one's tallness, which force one to always look down towards others not so tall, most likely, is to call such a soul to *inwardly come down* from his or her deceptive *high horse* with all that goes with it and live an uplifting humble life!

Fortunately our spiritual hero in this work, in the person of George Floyd at this auspicious End Time of judgement, with his elevated tall and huge *stature*, demonstrably lived a *humble life*, as was testified by friends and family and also seen in the video of the sad event!

Without any doubt, because of all the pervading spiritually *crippling* and dangerous dark radiations emanated and still emanating from all our loveless activities in many lifetimes, many natural happenings have been so beclouded that they have now lost their original values and meanings! Our God given abilities for *spiritual* discernment have thereby become considerably distorted and weakened if not totally lost! This has impaired our perceptions in *spiritual matters* above all else; causing that which is *intuitively* sensed to always be *erroneously* given a *physical* and hence *distorted* interpretations! Most disturbing is that it has continued to make it rather difficult for us to be able to understand and interpret the spiritual symbolism of our different statures in the way it is meant to be interpreted and utilised in our ongoing life's pursuits!—

When we then consider those of us who are neither tall nor short, we are presented with another visual picture that vividly mirrors the *spiritual* achievements of such human spirits. It is also a loving help to such individuals to have the picture of their own inner *lukewarmness* and *complacency* in spiritual aspirations and growth, constantly displayed before their inner gaze!

By this, they are *always reminded* that mediocrity, or being neither here nor there in their spiritual growth, reciprocally reflected physically in their stature, which is dictated by their obvious *half-hearted* application of the sublime love power towards their overall spiritual development, is inadvisable! Such attitude could very easily make them develop indolence of spirit, which would lead them to a more downward slide, to perdition; effected by, the primordial natural *law of spiritual gravity!* Therefore a more pronounced spiritual commitment to always function more rigorously in "*Living Love*", with heightened spiritual alertness and demonstrable upbuilding activities, is expected from those of us in this category of spiritual growth thermometer!

Sadly, one observes that the *vast majority* of mankind comes within this category! We who are of medium heights of various degrees, make up almost three quarters of the whole world population! This paints a *deplorable* spiritual picture on the whole, of the place mankind now *stands* and how regrettably little we have *progressed* in the expected *upward* direction in all these millions of years of human spiritual evolution!—

We have been lulled to *passivity* and complacency, bordering on the sleep of *spiritual death,* by the *little* we claim to know and do, like the Biblical five foolish virgins! Sadly, this milling great mass of humanity has unwittingly become this indolent, having succumbed to the bait of life of ease, comfort and pleasure; that assures living less exacting lives of striving to adjust to that which is expected of us for our own good!... It is more than time for us to wake up, if we really want to make it to the necessary spiritual finish line to which we are fated!!

Our only hope of fulfilling the *Will* of our Creator which cannot be circumvented, repudiated nor rejected by any creature, let alone us human spirits, lies in our making that necessary readjustment to living by the expression of *universal love* that governs all creation! There is no other way out! The laws of the universe, all which are only for our benefits, cannot be changed! We are the ones who must change our ways to meet God's *demands*, and He has mercifully given us all the aids for us so to do, crowned with these very *personal* ones!—

Let us examine the case of those who are still shorter than all the other human specimens above. We are aware that there are very many degrees of shortness of stature as there are of the other groups. Each stands as a *merciful* act of providing humanity one more obvious yardstick by which they can personally and visually measure their spiritual overall progress, from life time to life time!

Complementing those various degrees of tallness, those in this category of spiritual growth have reciprocally earned this mercy of *shortness*, to remind them to look far more *upwards* to God in their present lives, than they did in their past lives; for the same reason of fulfilling their spiritual purpose of existence, which they had regularly *short circuited* in many lives before! In their new lives such are to truly exert more energy doing so than they *model* looking up to their earthly partners; which is again a representation of the fact that, we have become sadly prone to physically interpreting and distorting all the spiritual realities of our lives!

As in all the other cases, this has also been *transmuted* and translated into a mere *physical* exuberance and *extroversion*, in the misguided effort to wrongly compensate for that which is *spiritually* lacking and urgently necessary for the required upward spiritual growth! That universally shared spiritual energy is so mercifully *compacted* in the small physical unit, ready for explosive application only in the right *upward* direction, through the expression of the values encoded in genuine unconditional sublime love; and not once again misguided and relegated to a mere physical *looking up* towards a partner, nor more often, in extroversion in exuberant compensatory mere physical acts, as generally exhibited by people in this category of spiritual statures, for material acquisition and worldly adoration!..

Fortunately for us, there is a merciful natural *mitigating force* that is *guaranteed* to bring about our being joyfully *lifted* out of any prevailing physical or spiritual predicaments, earned from the dark radiations of our spiritually none-acceptable acts at any time! This force can only be harnessed by us, and not by our Creator Who remains our benefactor and to Whom we are rightly accountable, for the obvious reason that: any of the unpleasant conditions that we may now find ourselves experiencing, is the retribution ignited only by our very own repeatedly bad and unacceptable spiritual *lifestyles* that have *reciprocally* justly accumulated from many lifetimes, including the present one; which have then been *mirrored* in our different *physical* statures! It therefore stands to reason to conclude that the only means of overcoming the justly *earned* predicament for all statures, lies in the *reactivation* of that which *unfailingly* generates the *liberating powerful force* of higher spiritual vibrations, brought about by the relentless application of *unconditional sublime Love* in all circumstances! This is guaranteed to flare up into the most luminous radiations our spirits can ever bring about, which is so badly needed for our peaceful coexistence resulting from our *spiritual* maturity, which consequently leads to our expected joyful accent to our spiritual home above!

We have no excuses for perpetuating all the evils that have been plaguing and threatening our existence since the world began! Because from the beginning, we were all purposefully equipped with the attributes of the powers of Divine Sublime Love; to help us uplift each other and make our world the projected joyous paradise on earth! Hence:

As a child you and I just wanted to be.
Nothing but just to be.
Nothing but to laugh and cry,
To play and smile.
Nothing but to be alive!
To jump around without a care,

And run around with no fear - -
Bringing joy to all around,
Softening mommy's and daddy's frowns!

We did not dream to be mobsters.
We did not dream to be gangsters.
Did not dream to be drug addicts,
Murderers or armed bandits!
Did not dream to be pimps,
Nor dream to be stinks
And beggars on the streets!
We did not dream to be homeless
Nor to be jobless and hopeless!

You and I did not want wars
Nor did we want to be bullied.
We wanted to make friends -
To hug and play in the rain,
Pick flowers in the planes
And fruits from plants;
Playing in the snow or sand,
Building castles and mansions
With our rioting imaginations!

We did not dream to be forgers
Nor to be impostors!
We did not dream to be terrorist,.
Anarchists,
Demi gods nor demagogues!....
You and I only wanted to be respected,

Valued and accepted. -
To be given a chance!....
Above all,
You and I wanted to love
And you to be loved!

Initially as stated above, our pure spirits *intuitively* only wanted to do what accords with the will of God. Unfortunately, as we grew up, through indoctrination by the society we assimilated the culture of *disregarding* the promptings of the intuition, instigated by our acquired over-developed and earth-bound intellect, which in most cases *completely* altered our perceptions and personalities. so much so that we no more bond easily as individuals or nations, but have become rather *suspicious* of one another, plotting and looking for ways to lord it over each other! As nations we do this with the show of our material supremacy and its attendant power, disregarding all the spiritual components in the *decisions* we make and the *procedures* we adopt in the building up of our individual and national or global empires; under which the labour forces and the unprivileged are at the greatest disadvantage! This is glaringly evident in the tragedy of the events in the case of George Floyd's murder and it's aftermath!

These discrepancies have created all the consequent atrocities now prevalent all round the world. The third world countries emulate their former imperial master nations in the *greed and exploitation* of their subjects. In doing all the above, we have pushed our fellowmen inescapably into resorting to deviant means and lifestyles that our *pure spirits as children* had not thought possible: Turning our world into a realm of desperation and perpetual conflict; rather than that of *peace and happiness*, that is willed by God; to which as children we were looking forward!

It is for the remembrance and reimplementation of the means to achieving the latter and much more that George Floyd's spirit opted to undertake the "Mission Karma"!

The highly volatile scenarios all over the world preceding George Floyd's' spiritual intervention is totally at variance with the expectations of our Creator and is dangerously heading us towards a disastrous end at this point in time! The brash audacity of taking other human being's lives as we do in all manners of wars, or on the pretext of fulfilling a duty as law enforcement officers anywhere in the world; constitutes the most outrageous affront to our Creator who gave us the imperative command that we *should not kill anyone!* "*Thou Shalt Not Kill*"! That we continue to blatantly do so as boldly demonstrated by Derek Chauvin and other supposed law enforcement officers, military forces and civilians round the world, is responsible for a lot of the karmic debts which we are bound to pay, individually and collectively, one way or another, now or later in the beyond, or back here on earth again! It is also the reason we are having to experience the escalating unfavourable - *retributive* reactions of the elements that are increasing in frequencies and magnitude daily simply everywhere!

The Original Plan

God being Love, Who made everything out of His Love, His only intention is for peace and joy to exist in all the worlds, brought about by the expression of sublime and unrelenting unconditional Love to all creatures on earth and especially from one man to another, no matter what the race, clime or status may be! This is because *Love is the integral ingredient* with which everything is made and also the *galvanising force* that controls everything that happens in the entire universe! The author of the one of a kind spiritual work mentioned many times before said that, I quote: "Everything is Love" and again He said : "Love governs all existence", therefore any alien force introduced in the play of events in Creation, invariably causes *a breach in the cosmic mechanism* that creates a calamitous problem in the execution and longed for accomplishment of the necessary spiritual set goals for all humanity as said earlier!

The obvious lack of the expression of this invaluable spiritual commodity of *Life Giving Love* without which everything in our world will eventually collapse; was starkly displayed in the process that led to George Floyd's murder. The same is at the root of other such atrocities committed especially against the underprivileged, systematically selected members of our societies of any colour!

The fact that loveless act of this nature – resurge now in the various forms that they did under the watches of famous historic emperors, popes, kings and other rulers of the world: Bring home the *significance* of the Mission Karmic act of George Floyd seeking to help liberate mankind from the retributive bonds of the threads of our repeated evils that are now heading us to our destruction at this "End Time"!

The said mission drove home how enormous the benefit derived from the service to his fellowmen is, in his decision to psychically prompt us all to reexamine ourselves, with regards to opting *to love* rather than *to hate*, which diverts us from pursuing our true purpose for existing on earth! Our *right choice* will help us effect the necessary changes that will make our actions accord with the requirements of the Laws and Will of our Maker. That alone, and not any material intervention, derived from inventions and other highbrow scientific breakthroughs, can help us do so!

The repeated allusion in this work to *Love* is because it is a sublime virtue that embraces or encompasses *all that is good* and compassionate. In His mission as the personification of God's Divine Love in creation, Jesus strove to resurrect the Love we had buried; letting us know that the only way to fulfil His Father's *adamantine* Will, is to Love God first with all our heart, soul and body, which will lead us to doing what is *good* to everyone in our world. That's why He told us —

To "love your neighbours as yourself",
And do unto them as we would
Like it done to us!
Loving our neighbours as we love ourselves:
Christians, Jews, Muslims and the rest,
We would want to know best
That which unites us,
Not that which divides us
Nor what incites us!

Loving our neighbours as we love ourselves -
We would want to know best,
What helps the other grow,
Not what makes him unable to play his role
For mankind as a whole!
We would want to know

What makes the other's life sparkle,
Not what keeps him in shackles
And makes him buckle.

Loving our neighbours as we love ourselves:
Christians, Jews, Muslims and the rest;
We would want to know best,
What makes the other shine -
Not what covers him in slime!
We would want to supply
What makes the other thrive,
Not what causes his decline
And inclined to crimes!

Loving our neighbours as we love ourselves:
We would want to know best-
What makes the other happy,
Not what increases his apathy!
We would want to give
What helps the other win -
Not what makes him lose and cringe
Like a bird that lost its wings
In a battle he could not win!

Loving our neighbours as we love ourselves,
Christians, Jews, Muslims and the rest ,
We would want to know best,
What helps the other succeed!
Not what makes his dreams cease
We would help each other
Make the world better ,
And our lives safer!
Letting George Floyd also "Breathe"!

Why George Floyd

Loving our neighbour as we love ourselves,
We would preserve all lives!
The flora and fauna
Six footed or more
Chirping, gliding, crawling, or hissing; they all belong!
We would share nature's bounty
Living and letting others live -
Letting George Floyd "Breathe"!

Defection, Addiction and Depression!

From all what is transpiring in our societies round the world, it is obvious that we have forgotten the original plan and brushed aside or simply abandoned all the mentoring parts we as parents, brothers and sisters, elders, educators, employers, rulers, religious leaders and the like, in short, the parts all the members and groups of the human race should have been playing all along, for achieving that *set spiritual goal!*

Which can only be done by following the tenets of a spiritual oriented society! In its place, we have continuously only sought to exploit our gifts for *selfish* ends, plundering and ceasing others' where-with-all with impunity, leaving them despondent and deprived of power let alone sustenance; brandishing selfishness on our family crests, while everyone else is trampled down! By so doing we have turned our world upside down and *counterfeited* our images of Him who made us!

We now look much more like clowns,
Garbed in flamboyant gowns,
Mimicking each other in a suicidal dance,-
Like brainwashed devotees in a trance!
Our original saintly selves bound
And gagged in uniforms and gowns
Which boost our egocentric forms
Our cruelty displayed with force
In the torture of such as George Floyd!
The officers paraded and gloated,
In our power mongering pursuits!

Our corrupted ego in this remiss,

Sees the world with on
The material isles,
For the intellect, said so -
Stranding our spirits in desolation!
Cutting off our ability
To be who we really are!
Clamping us down
With the iron fist of sagacity,
The delusion of grandeur,
The wine of opulence
And the caviar of spiritual indolence!

The result is that we only amass and clutter our lives with irrelevant ideologies which drown our spirit within, cramping it in the same manner as hoarders *bury themselves* under heaps of their *irrelevant* acquisitions!

To make matters even worse, we are not aware that the Love energy which flows into us from above for our emotional and moral sustenance every split second of our lives, twenty four seven, is meant to be *unceasingly* utilised for upbuilding purposes at all times! If not, just like a river whose path is blocked would find other outlets, the said energy would be compelled to do the same, by causing a diversion of its *motivating* power to *spiritually destructive* pursuits; such as love of sex, smoking, drinking, gambling, and other pursuits to which we most times become *addicted!* —

The addiction becomes inevitable because of the pressure of the influx of the energy in question, which mounts up within us and compels continuous expression to *avoid* stagnation in Creation! Continuous movement being one of the Primordial Laws of Creation!...The supply being ever constant, therefore, it demands constant outlets! Being also so inexhaustible, it cannot be constrained nor restricted, but *must be* distributed and shared with all that exists at all times to avoid any stagnations!

There is yet another danger in our *hoarding* or withholding our given flow of the sublime Love energy. That danger lies in its irrepressible manner of operation which we have *no power* to change, control or limit! We are by it, spiritually compelled to dispense it as it flows unceasingly to us!

Meaning that the love dispensed *unceasingly* to us by our Maker, is to be passed on unceasingly too, and not to be spent sporadically and above all, not on only one person! .

If we do, the *unexpended* influx would *congeal* and go stale within us, driving us to become sour and irritable, our moods to swing from one extreme to another, displaying what is then termed *bi-polar* disorder symptoms! Besides our relationship with our only chosen one, may become *possessive* if not even oppressive!

Another dreadful outcome of being stingy with the energy of Love is that the unused influx having congealed, will *further* make us frigid, moody and even lethargic! We could even easily lose contact with reality, because we feel ever so lonely and *isolated from people*, believing that everything is against us and nothing is working out for us; plunging us into the much dreaded *depression*!

The depression is actually the reaping of our inability to share the love we have received with others. Because, in the due automatic response of the Law of Reciprocal Action, nature has then *held back* what it has *reciprocally* created for us as our due rewards! This conforms to the reasoning that we cannot reap where we have not sown, as dictated and executed by the natural Law of existence!

Globally therefore, our failure in carrying out our duty of expressing unconditional love whole-heartedly to others, has put us all in a *confrontational* position with the cardinal Law of the universe, which is the Law of universal Love. Our only salvation from all our troubles politically or socially, lies in our accepting that *failure*, realising that we have no other alternative than to let the Love energy *flow out* of us unto other people and things in and around our various geographical and geopolitical environments; through our behaviours and policies, in our various present governmental systems; right to whatever chores or duties as individual citizen we have to perform at home and in the community at large anywhere we may be!

When this does not happen, humans suffer *emotional* neglect and abandonment and many psychological problems which lead them to all manners of misdemeanours, and to social and political destabilisations, riots and even wars! At the private individual level, resorting to the comforts of *artificial aids* like the inseminations of drugs of all types just to numb their rioting nerves!

George Floyd *succumbed* to the application of some form of palliative for the same reason of numbing the negative experiences he was having with the insensitive indifference and lovelessness of the powers that kept him down and oppressed him and people like him! This is one of the evils he had spiritually chosen to help eradicate with the " Mission Karma"!

The Dangers of Ignoring The Small Voice

Intuition is our much undervalued and *ignored* spiritual ability that *supersedes* that of the sagacious earth-bound intellect of the frontal brain which should be under our spirit's control! It is that which is meant to direct all our activities spiritually with impressions from the sola-plexus, via the now *shrunken* small brain earlier described as the cerebellum! This most devastating shrinking of the back brain was due to the overdevelopment of the intellect, as said before, which has sadly left mankind spiritually very much dysfunctional; operating disappointedly only as *caricatures* of ourselves!

Most people in the mundane law enactment and their dutiful enforcement, have fallen into the trap of this most distorting predicament. Watching Derek Chauvin and the other police officers' actions, looked like watching a *scary* fantasy movie scene, with *unreal* human caricatures, doing what breathing *real life* humans *should not ever do* to one another! By-standers stood horrified and agape, mesmerised, and in shocking disbelief of their very own eyes as to the existential impactful extent we have *distorted* our souls!

Many such scenes pervade our societies everywhere and truly make one fear for our future safety! It is therefore no wonder that with a spiritual foresight, spirits like George Floyd, do any thing they can, to arrest the continuous perpetration of such heinous spiritual and physical offences that continue to cause the prevention of our advancement to the maturity we seek!

Under normal circumstances, the indispensable spiritual tool of the intuition functions un-intrusively:

Like a radar,
Scanning all acts
Before they hatch,
To inform us the right ways to speak
Or not to speak,
To think or not to think -
To do just everything!

But often we fail to heed its gentle voice
And shut it up with an intellectual choice!
Our corrupted egos now do not care
To see the warning glares
Of the volcanic flares
From the mountains of our mistakes
Gathering the forces of high seismic strength!

Our corrupted egos now do not listen
To that small still voice inside the prisons
We built with self-pride,
And fortified with vain rights!
Our gagged intuition,
Not able to function,
Stunt all our operations:

Making it difficult to have the recognition
Nor the volition
To let Love drive all our actions!
Shunning all that shun its injunctions
On policies devoid of Love
That make us turn blind eyes to loveless acts;

Uwa Udensi Hunwick

Implanting injustices in all life's tracks - -

Making us combat with the Loving Force
That galvanised all forms
With sublime creative glue,
For our survival in all weather!
Subverting our own true nature,
Degrading our given valour,
Subjecting us to squirming victims!
Vices now hold us down
Making it difficult to wear crowns
Of victory over all the odds
That want to make us fall
From the pinnacles of joy
For successes in all our ploys
In our spiritual toils !

We continue to discriminate and incite divisiveness and all forms of *hatred* that lead to acts of violence as we witness daily all round the globe, with people rising against various oppressive governing bodies and agencies. Our *intellectual* approach to life, has made us unable to see that we need to rise above the *earthly* conceptions *only* for solutions to our endemic problems, which are intrinsically *spiritual* in origin! This should be *decisive* in our policy making as nations or individuals, considering that none of what we are expertly propounding in our intellectually derived proposals, are what our spirits want nor need for the achievement of the one thing we all came to earth to do!

But the basic fact that we are not truly aware of who we are and what we are doing here on earth, which militates against our ability to proceed *resolutely* in the only way that will lead to the unequivocal successful attainment of that our assigned spiritual goal; needs to be finally resolved sooner than later, because we don't have anymore time. We are in the Biblical prophesied "*End Time*"

George Floyd must have become aware of this in his past life, which culminated in his making the decision to take the step he then took in this life. We all also choose to make different decisions before reincarnating, most of which are structured for our personal spiritual progress specifically, while others, like George Floyd's, are for the general upbuilding of present day humanity in one specific spiritual way or another! Most likely, Martin Luther King and others, must have done that!

This is obviously because everything that happens to anyone or any group of people of any particular race or country, in our human existence; is spiritually based and preplanned in the long time march of events before and after reincarnation! Nothing ever comes from nothing!

Who We Are And What We Are To Be Doing

The failure to live up to the expectations and challenges of being made and equipped with the tools to develop into the likenesses of the Image of God, is traceable mainly to two things: One is not knowing the true origin and therefore the nature of the various *bundles* of incessantly vibrating *love energy* particles, commonly identified exteriorly as *man*! The other is not being aware of the inherent *self implicating* nature of his said mandatory spiritual evolution and development on this earth! However, if God originated everything out of Himself, man's origin and spiritual obligations are obvious and do not need any further elaboration.

Just as an egg of a butterfly evolves and matures, in the same manner does the entity known as man, whose eager spirit in the form of a seed-grain, set out on its granted *spiritual* evolutionary journey towards maturity on earth eons ago, from its original home above; in the well structured pure and impeccable evolutionary process discussed earlier.

Symbolically this very unique process is now preserved in that which usually takes place physically and also spiritually throughout the very early period of pregnancy, right from gestation to birth, and continues to the time man takes his first steps toward his much needed physical as well as spiritual maturity!

Spiritually, the evolving man is defined first as a *spirit spark* out of the radiation of the *Holy Spirit* of the Trinity, Who is the pure personification of the Divine *embodiment* of the "*spiritual*" essence of the energy particles of the *Will* of God! It is He, Who as the *executive* personality of God, stands to carry out all of God's Will in His creating, sustaining and ruling of the universe, Who it is said that, in the very beginning, He allegorically walked on the surface of the waters to create all that there is; as was reported in the Old Testament account of the biblical genesis of all that exists in creation!—

Hence the evolving man, first emanated from the *Holy Spirit* , as a *spirit* spark that successively evolved from a *spirit* seed-grain, into a *spirit*-germ, and then further into a developing spiritual entity, that is *fully* endowed with all the undeveloped attributes of God's own Divine Living Love power and characteristics: all which were further encapsulated in the cloak called the soul; which then finally wears the *human body*, after the very well orchestrated long processes of the evolution described earlier, during which it had been acquiring *layers of functional* outer coverings, from all the higher and lighter realms that exist, on its necessary descent to the material *denser* realm of life;- far away from *paradise* its only spiritual home. The last outer covering of the acquired *physical* human body, is for the practical purposes of both being *visible*, and capable of *physically functioning* in the last supportive evolutionary environment, of the dense *physical* earth; where it does not belong, but must reside for a period of time, for the *attainment* of the designated spiritual goal.

During its time on earth, it is expected to fully deploy all its endowed love based spiritual abilities to enable it/him gain full consciousness of his prescribed responsibilities towards his Creator; only to be attained via his *love base* services to his fellowmen. To fulfill this injunction, he is required to put all the *upbuilding attributes of the Love within him to full use*, in order that all along the way, he will derive the supreme happiness that their dutiful and right applications for ever offer!

Those who have adopted the Christian faith may remember the parable of the *fate* of the servant who was kindly given the talents to multiply, but who failed to do so by rather *hiding* them! Those who of other faiths can easily conjecture what the well meaning master would have done to the wilful disobedient servant!.

Such displeasing and disingenuous acts are prevalent in the world today, making a lot of us accomplices in the atrocious dissatisfying practices that are *spiritually* unproductive and consequently obstructive to our overall spiritual development! And it is about eradicating this that a" *Mission karma*" like that of George Floyd at this crucial time in our ordained *spiritual* evolutionary stage is critical! Because it *highlights* the discrediting result of our neglected spiritual responsibility of going forth into the world with our given " *talents* " *of Love*…to love others as we love ourselves! If Derek Chauvin and others like him invested their endowed talents of love in the execution of their daily duties, what he did to George would not have happened!

If we really want to stop such happening again and again, our attitudes towards one another need to change, and with all the abilities with which we are endowed, strive harder to understand the *spiritual nature* of our existence, which will not fail to compel all of us to *focus all our attention* and pursuits in the spiritual direction. This will guarantee our freedom from repeated earth lives on the designated spiritual school, where sadly up till now, we have all *sheepishly* mostly pursued our material development only! In so doing we have dangerously *neglected our duties* to our *own spirits* that set out on the search for their development in the first place; otherwise we would not be here at all! Think of that seriously.

To further shed light on who we really are and what we are meant to be doing here on earth, the following metaphor may paint the *right picture*. Imagine that the United Nations cared so much for humanity that it harnessed all its powers and resources to prepare the moon as a suitable *temporary* habitat for mankind. Not as a frivolous holiday resort but for fulfilling the profound and burning desire for improvement of the less active or unproductive members of the world's society, whose talents could *only blossom* in such a unique environment. After their temporary sojourn and training they are transported back to earth to then *"fit in"*… Imagine what necessary preparations would be made and how they would look!

During their time of sojourn, they would be known as moon- folks, heavily garbed in their strange looking weatherised, protective and environmentally functional moon-cloaks that are vital for the success of their mission. Keeping that picture in mind, as we retrace our origin and purpose here on earth: In place of the United Nations, substitute *God*!

In place of the earth humans going to the moon, substitute *spirit beings*, initially known as spirit grains and germs, because they were not yet developed but longing to do so. These then having to be sent to earth which God had lavishly prepared exclusively as their designated *"spiritual school of Love"* The school is equipped with all the tools they would need for the full blossoming of all their Living Love potentials through practical application, whose results would give them supreme joy, peace and eternal happiness!—

In place of the birth place of the moon folks as Africa, America, Asia, Australia or Europe, substitute *Paradise - "Heaven"*, the birth-place and home of all the spirit germs. In place also of the environmentally adapted moon-cloaks, which anchors the comparably lighter bodies of the moon-folks from earth on the alien moon surface, substitute the evolved human body; which is also environmentally adapted to anchor the very *light* spirit beings on the alien dense earth. The reason being the fact that as a spirit, it is composed of very light, fine and invisible energy particles of the essence of love that is weightless!

Remember the creation of the earthly body of the first man in the Bible, with the spirit being God's biblical metaphoric *breath*! As such and being *invisible*, it is by far much lighter than the body that harbours and anchors it in then denser atmosphere and environment of the material dense earth! The purpose, though strictly spiritually oriented, eternal and suffused with Divine love, is the same as that metaphorically intended by the United Nations.

Were we the spirit germs, longing for development prepared for the spiritual journey and temporary settlement? The creation and evolutionary stories point to this truth and the practical and comprehensive spiritual book mentioned before, gives a full account of the spiritual preparations and subsequent journeys of all the spirit germs through many expansive spiritual realms down to material earth for the intended development!

With all good intentions so far however, much has developed physically, *not spiritually*, which is sadly in the *opposite* direction of that which was originally planned; creating a sad cosmic imbalance that has bred what is *spiritually* as anti-*productive as it is obstructive* to the true overall progress of all mankind; duly precipitating the unnerving cosmic crisis that is now rapidly unravelling before all of us!...— This is evident in the chaotic and disasterous events that are taking place in many areas of our lives all over the world!

Proofs Of Being Spirits

But how does one really know that one is truly a spirit that is sojourning here on earth far away from Paradise its only true home, to which it is to return at the end of its successful schooling, since one cannot see the spirit? Could that not be the core factor that plays into our inability to comprehend the purpose of its existence, let alone its relevance in life itself? Here are a few every day tell-tale questions and other insights to consider in this regard:—

At night when one dreams, what is that entity which *leaves* one's body which is lying limp in bed to be engaged in all those sometimes weird adventures far away from the bed? Sometimes it goes far back in time and at other times it is projecting unimaginable and daring experiences and global happenings far into the distant future; (popular psychological propositions with trade jargons and terms not withstanding) - visiting strange places, performing strange feats like flying, etc. etc? And even if per chance it is the projection of one's wishful thoughts as acclaimed experts may claim, *who or what* is actually acting out those wishes while one is fast asleep, well garbed in one's day clothing, or sometimes in one's birthday- suit?… And what about the existence of ghosts that some of us can see occasionally, of some very unfortunate earthbound human spirits, perhaps in need of some redress or assistance of one type or another for earthly perceived unsolved issues! Does one *have* a conscience? Where is it located in the human anatomy? Is the mind concrete and visible? Does one *have* intuition? Again is it visible and tactile? And where is one's will power in the said anatomy? In spite of all of that, one's spirit possesses all these none physical *spiritual* components!

The spirit is subtle, invisible and *immortal*, *schooling* on earth through the instrument of the physical body as illustrated in the analogy of the Moon-folk, without which it can only float about and be unable to make any contact with anything in the environment of the denser tactile earth for the required training!

From time to time however, it is obliged to withdraw from the earthly covering at death, whether or not it has fulfilled its purpose of development. Conveniently for us ever bungling humanity however, out of the infinite Love and Omniscience of the Creator, we as human spirits are additionally given a merciful window of undeserved grace in the Love motivated mechanism of *reincarnation*! In a nutshell, this happening takes effect in the following manner.

Because of the Divine Purity of the Creator, by the law of homogeneity- *like attracting like*, the prevailing low vibrations and dark insidious radiations that issue from our repeated failures, can never penetrate beyond material Creation to the realm of all Light! This creates an *impenetrable* barrier between the light pervaded Paradise and now darkened earth, which lies at an unfathomable distance far below that pure spiritual home of man, towards which we are meant to rise ultimately! Consequently, in His Omniscient Love, mercy and grace, the perfect workings of the law of *homogeneity*, automatically sets in to ensure the happening of the following: Any physically and newly departed *immature* human spirit, who in the course of the earth life just left, had been quite *complacently apathetic* to its responsibility of maintaining high and sublime spiritual values, governed by sublime Love, which only radiates light; faces an automatic temporary but insurmountable spiritual problem of vibrational incompatibility with the Light, which immediately bars further progress upwards towards its home in Paradise! —

His past overall deviant loveless conducts would have left him totally ill prepared for ascent into the light regions meant for mature spirits that he was hoping for; being hampered by his *non-homogeneous luminous* upward driving radiations! Such an unfortunate newly departed spirit cannot consequently be homogeneously attracted to rise magnetically beyond all of material Creation, which is polluted with all manner of dark radiations and detrimental forms of lovelessness, to which he had contributed!

In the provision of God's eternal Love however, any such spirit is then permitted to *reincarnate* to resume it's spiritual schooling in Living Love applications! This can either take place in the already polluted earth homogeneous to it, or be constrained to remain in the also polluted immediate area of the beyond for a certain period of time for its very necessary reorientation. Such a spirit as said, strictly *debars* himself from proceeding to Heaven!

Therefore by the operation of God's adamantine laws, which Jesus said He didn't come to break, one of which is the active aforementioned Law of Homogeneity: It is *homogeneously highly impossible* for the blood of the Divine personage, Who for ever casts and generates the most luminous Light in all of Creation, highly impossible for it to be used to counteract the effect of the *dark* radiations emanating from our unrighteous, loveless lifestyles! The *Will* of God, manifested in the natural laws of Creations stipulates, that we can only do our cleansing strictly by ourselves! That is why Jesus said that He will not pay heed to all those who incessantly call His name, but only to those who "*do*" His Father's *Will*, which governs all creation and is permanently encapsulated in the eternal law of Sublime Living Love, which He personified; and its expression of which is the only way back to paradise for all humanity!

Unfortunately for the defaulting departed human spirit, his initial reorientation courses may have to take place in a less favourable environment, which he formed for himself while on earth with his loveless acts! The degree and nature of the popularly alluded unpleasantness of the new environment, commonly referred to as "*hell*"; is in perfect justice, commensurate experientially, to the said spirit's accrued retributive symbolic forms spiritually created by his ill practices while on earth!...

God, Who is Love and does not know pain nor evil, cannot allow nor create any pain nor Hell for us to go to suffer in everlasting tortures of all descriptions!

It is helpful to bear in mind that everything we do in our lives with our radiated creative rays of love energy particles, under the perpetual life releasing pressure from the Divine Creative Force, is mandated by their inherent *creative* abilities; , to *take forms* here on earth for us to see and benefit from, and in the beyond, for us to experience and review the life just completed; for the benefit of our future lives' remedial attempts!

These intensified *mirror* images of our past earthly actions, are induced to take their spiritual identical forms by the strength and nature of the radiations issued from the vibrations of the said earthly actions, magnetically transmitted into identical areas in the beyond. This *magnetic* attraction also serves the departed spirit as a means for his deserved pull by higher forces out of matter to its *self* made hell, or joyfully to Paradise, or back to earth as the case may be.

However, a disturbing condition for the immediately departed spirit occurs, if his attachment and the initial immediate pull back to earth proves to be extreme and deemed urgent by him for one reason or another. More often than not, it may be due to the pressing desire to seek redress or forgiveness for anyone of a sundry loveless acts committed against him or her or that which he or she had committed against other people or against himself, say in his overindulgences in food, drinking or smoking, sex, etc.,

Some disturbing aspects of this have recently been lightly explored by conscientious artists in movies such as "Ghost" "The Frighteners" and in a onetime television series, "Ghost Whisperers" and the like. These honest attempts at looking at some aspects of the after-life as it really is, however minimal, is encouraging and perhaps could have been taken more seriously if we had not abandoned ourselves to the beguiling illusion of intellectual superciliousness in these matters!.

The perfection of the said spiritual conveyance mechanism for departed spirits in the beyond, is the means by which the nature of the radiations of our earthly activities enable us to be magnetically pulled *step by step* after death out of all matter and up to heaven or if not, repeatedly back to earth for reincarnation or to hang in the troublesome state of being between and betwixt! We are categorically not transported by the blood of Jesus to heaven as is conveniently believed by many Christians!

To our greatest disadvantage and disfavour, this false teaching heavily *contributes* to the overall spiritual delinquency, laxity and self-complacency now prevalent in our society today. It undeniably encourages blasphemous acts among *acclaimed* believers; giving room for the irresponsible, immoral and insensitive life that is now prevalent. Such is what has led to the audacity of the *heinous* treatments given to our fellow human spirits all over the world; exemplified in the like given to George Floyd and others in different countries by so called believers!

We do that, believing that no matter what we do to anyone, the assumed propitiatory sacrifice of Jesus, *atones* for our sins before God! Where as it exposes the fact that our fervent avowal of being followers of Christ is greatly faulted by the propagation of wrong doctrines which only encourage our hypocritical Christian candidature to those who *talk the talk* but don't *walk the walk!*

If we remotely did, George Floyd, Briana Taylor and a million and more others like them would be alive today! There would have been no more wars, and many other atrocities we commit everyday as individuals and as nations. All these would have ceased and our world would have become a resemblance of our spiritual home of *paradise*. But deluding themselves as most Christians do, with the notion of acquittal of transgressions against God's commands, by simply believing in the blood of Jesus, has poisoned our chances of ever fulfilling one of the facts about *"reaping what we sow"* as He himself taught mankind! It has made us susceptible to living spiritually *irresponsible* lives which is the cause of our *decadence* and severe spiritual backslides. The crucifixion of our Lord Jesus Christ was a dastardly loveless act committed against the personified Love of God Himself, Who did no evil and Who said *"You shall reap what you sow"*! Did He reap what He sowed? Did He kill anyone?! Yet a lot of believers live with the delusion of immediate return to His arms, as if in conclusive reciprocity for what good seeds they have spiritually sown with their lives!

In reality what rather happens is, as we sin and commit acts of disobedience to His Father's irrevocable laws, *"we"* and only we ourselves, *not* Jesus stand to bear the consequences of our actions! No one else can do that for any human spirit of any religious conviction or none! This is so for the simple reason that it is an immutable operational primordial law of all of Creation which cannot be circumvented, erased, repudiated nor *altered* even by a hair's breath!

Jesus did not sin and did not need to *pay for what He did not do*! If He sinned in any way or form, He would have been contradicting His own teachings and disobeying His Father whose Holy adamantine Will He came all the way from the Divine realm to physical earth to reinstate! He came down at a great *sacrifice of His Divinity*, into a world that had become cut off from the Light of His Father, primarily because of the lovelessness of their lifestyles, He being the *personification* of Sublime Love!

That we are so self-complacent in the face of our crass spiritual depravity, which is the inevitable fallout of our obstinacy and disobedience, induced by our blind adherence and complete dependency on the sagacious and overdeveloped intellect that is eternally only materially oriented and, undeniably speeding us on our way to perdition; is why caring human spirits like our hero George Floyd took the drastic step of doing what he considered would jerk us up from our stupor, before it is too late for a majority of us!

Reincarnation Destinations

For ensuring the *atonement and reorientation* of our recalcitrant human spirits to living spiritually upbuilding lives in our next incarnations, all departed human spirits are transported not just to anywhere in the beyond, but typically to the realm of kindred defaulting spirits undergoing the gruesomeness of their orientation drills, or to alike people in behaviour and propensities back here on earth, even if of races different from the one to which they last belonged!

Fostering this unavoidable happening is the natural law of the *attraction of homogeneous species*, which induces us in our next incarnations to be attracted to situations and circumstances similar to that which led to our failures in the expression of the various forms of *Sublime Living Love* during the life we previously led. This affords us the wonderful liberating windows of opportunities to redeem ourselves! Because it gives us a most spiritually needed and convenient chance to subconsciously *revisit* our mistakes in their familiar context and circumstances, so we can strive to recognise them and become more conscious of living in *the express Will* of our Creator in all the ways we failed to do in our past lives!

We therefore need to be very mindful of discriminations in any given form in any of our new locations. For instance, if we are now located in Africa, a Chinese immigrant could have been *an African* before!

By another aforementioned Primordial Natural Law of existence which is the *Law of Reciprocal Action* and therefore ensures that we reap what we have sown:, former emperors and rulers of the world and former slave owners throughout human history conversely could themselves, by the workings of that law now be slaves or descendants of slaves and vice- versa anywhere in the world including the Americas!

Again most people who are now seen to be experiencing terrible hardships in some *very poor and underdeveloped* parts of our world today, could have themselves created the conditions they now face in previous lives, by not meeting the requirements of living with Love in so many different ways! Such would be said to be reaping what they had previously sown.... *We all are*, in this present life! —

All the above demonstrate how generously and graciously you and I, as developing human spirits are amply given what we need to help us readjust our lives to the demands of the just and loving adamantine laws of Creation in the perfect orchestration of its love based mechanism. *Unfulfilled*, sad and disappointed with himself or herself should any human spirit be, who through spiritual self denial, allows his or herself to become continuously and *counter* productively attached to dark threads of radiations from loveless acts through the *obsessive* pursuance of all what is only material, to the total negligence of that which was meant to lead to our spiritual freedom and maturity.

Because all existence is totally a spiritual undertaking, which is *piloted and controlled* by its said automatic Sublime Love based operational mechanism, all that do not comply with the designated system, are duly and ultimately rejected and pulled downwards and away from the spiritual source which is in The Light of God, that leads to the perpetually longed for achievement of the designated *spiritual* goal!—

That is what we regularly struggle to avoid by reincarnating over and over again anywhere in the world; where we may have the subconsciously craved opportunities of making amends and reforming our lives to achieve our full potentials in becoming the befitting spiritual entities, meant to develop their sacred inherent potentials as candidates of the *Likeness of God's Image!*

This manifestation of the Likeness of God's Holy Image in our life styles which leads to our acquisition of spiritual maturity, is what must have motivated Spirits like George Floyd to have strove in past lives to acquire the spiritual growth, which in this lifetime manifest in their *elevated heights*, like those giants of earliest mankind on earth. Notably in stark contrast to most of the *spiritually delinquent* crowds of people of today, that make up more than three-quarters of the human population; who are grossly self-complacent: earning us the spiritual *physical* reminder of the reciprocated *medium* heights at best!

It is useful to remember that when we newly incarnated and more spiritually connected, living simpler and more natural wholesome lives, we were all much taller. In fact, findings by archeologists have confirmed this with the discoveries of fossils of skulls and skeletons of gigantic proportions in some ancient sites in some parts of the world!

Spiritual Food

We need to *feed* our human *spiritual* inner core with *spiritual* food, just as we feed our physical bodies and for the same reason. Since we don't do that, the majority of the earth's population as stated before, is now made up of human spirits who have stunted themselves with *spiritual malnutrition*: — Because as previously said, all the things we do take on forms that metaphorically *nourishes* us *spiritually* as well as physically. We all now spiritually look like victims of wars in refugee camps, or of starved victims of long devastating famine by the unloving attitude we have developed, which continues to militate against us. The debilitating and numbing *effect of the starvation* which the spirit has undergone through the ages, is now crowned with a death dealing apathy and insensitivity! Evidently, some of us have become so numbed and spiritually impervious that we can treat our fellow human beings the way George Floyd was treated!

It has also made us develop *devious* ways for survival in a sad world deluged with caterers of the self, where we struggle to metaphorically live in a global *spiritual refugee camp*; in which we are forced to device all means of manipulative ploys for gaining access to what we desperately need! This has lead us to the development of many vices as listed below and more, which have equally led to our treatments of one another in ways that are unexpected of true human spirits like Derek Chauvin and all humanity who should know that:

Racial discrimination is a vice,
Which incites hatred and crimes;
And not the nature of Love:
For Love loves all!
Should know -
That to malign is a vice,

Uwa Udensi Hunwick

Which promotes disputes and of strife;
And not the nature of Love -
For Love breathes peace and joy
And keeps death in defeat

Should know -
That to be Bigotry is a vice
That wears the hat of pride,
Against the natures of Love -
For Love is shy!
Should know -
That greed is a vice
Which cheats and exploits,
And not the nature of Love -
For Love is altruistic!

Should know -
That violence and aggression
Plague man with fatal crisis,
And not the nature of Love;
For Love loves its kind!
Should know -
That rudeness and crudity
Turn people into brutes!
Not at all the nature of Love -
For love wears the crown of Grace!

Should know -
That a bragger is a liar.
It feeds vanity

But love breaths humility:
The true nature of Love. –
The elixir of life!
Without Love, is without Life!
To be divisive is a vice
That fans disunity and caprice
And not the nature of Love!
For love unites
Ties the ribbon on the flowers
And waters them with love
In the true nature of a human being.
That knows, that to be despotic is a vice
That sponsors oppression:
Which puts progress in recession!
And not the nature of Love,
Nor that of a true human being -
In the likeness of the Image of God!

For the success of our common *spiritually mandated* goal, there are existential abilities and qualities that define and validate every human spirit as hinted above, which subconsciously guide every one of us in everything we do...! — So long as we are Spirits in human forms, you and I are subconsciously motivated to strive to develop into the "Likeness of the Image of God". But now in our various intellectually *misguided* ways we have become crassly impervious to the promptings of our indwelling spirits! Nevertheless, the truth remains that we are all here on earth subconsciously striving to do the same thing! —

That terribly mishandled inherent spiritual sublime *loving* desire, is not for its carnal appeal to which it has been shamelessly relegated, but categorically *is* for enabling each other to subliminally and physically achieve our common spiritual only goal of attaining spiritual consciousness and maturity!

George Floyd had obviously been striving to do this in his own way in other incarnations, just like you and I have ben trying to do the same. This time however, he reincarnated with the "Mission Karma" to *buttress* our collective dream of redemption from the vices some of which are sited above, that have been preventing us and choking our lives as he was symbolically choked to death in that memorable loveless act of Derek Chauvin!

Could we but always remember the spiritual significance of it all, his mission would not be in vain and:

All our struggles will not be in vain.
'Cause we are equipped to the teeth,
To pass Love's baton with no slack:
From hand to hand,
Track to track.-
To red, black, white or yellow,
Lighting the paths for all to follow-
Strong and bold to win the race,
With love on smiling faces!

But man has sabotaged his own survival game!
Putting himself in constant fear,
Putting himself in dire defence,
Lacking the protective strength
Of nature's bonding man with another,
Neighbour and another,
Clan and another,
Political group and another,
Religious group and another!

Family bonds now hang on the balance -
Members lost in the avalanche
Of wars of survival of the fittes!t

Little love now lost in the tempest
Between one party and another,
One nation and the other!...
Plots and counter plots hatched -
Making the world a battle ground
Of bedazzled antelopes staggering around

Weak-kneed with their dreams!
Groping for water in foaming vistas
Glimpsed through tinted political and religious screens
Contorting and distorting every scene -
Perverting everything gleaned,
Destroying the reality of sanity!..,
Compelled to step on each other's toes,
Striking each other down with bigoted blows
Because the dreams they had faded in the haze!

Driving them to fabricate and castigate,
Degrade, humiliate and intimidate
Each other in the recurring fight
To regain their lost human rights
In the strangled spiritual strife:
Which has made our
Tomorrow dark and blank!..
Nothing satisfying the struggling man
Anxious to break the invisible hand

That holds him back
From taking firm stands
To escape from our self-made traps!
Yes we all set the traps,

By the powers we wield

That make the world bleed.

Hate and prejudice fanning the flames-

As we move and grope about in chains!

Nothing, calming our ravaged nerves!

Some of us then turn to opioids in desperation, to sooth their gnawing pains just like George who succumbed to the temptation in his weakest moment. For nothing was healing the gnawing wounds in his and the wombs of the aspiring youths of bruised humanity, burdened with the yoke of over the top *self-pride*, bagged with the claim of the *superiority* of strands of favoured humanity!... Yet we were all " *created equal*" and were meant to feel equal!—

Contradicting this holy edict in various manmade cliques, has definitely shot-circuited progress in all of known human developmental processes and fanned the now raging flame of discrimination, recriminations and discontent with all their attendant banes; triggering *of the deluge* of not only the trending justified rebellions of oppressed humanity but also that of retributive natural disasters in place of the cosmic fruits of joyous peace and happiness reciprocally reaped from the seeds of *unconditional sublime Love* sown in all the fields of human activities!

The Napoleonic and Hitlerian complexes, resurge here and there unabated in our world's heads of states who are cast in those same *vain* moulds, with their egos out of control, and completely aware of the turmoil they would unleash, as the general populace react to their ploys in the manipulation of their consciences for self-interests only, rousing all the hidden *negative* sentiments bred from centuries of ill-bred and loveless societies otherwise:—

Why brew bigoted views

Of who is black and who is not,

If not to break the natural bond

And divide and rule the clinging mob?

Why who is brown and who is not,

If not to diffuse the sublime union
And plant separatism as a winning ruse?

A brazen show of power abuse,
A jaundiced attempt to defuse
And contradict the bonds of love
That links one human to the other?
A blatant, senseless seizure of power
From the gentle hands of Love!
That formed and governs all that exist!

'Now racism has dug a deep pit
And set the mark for winning the race!
For all the human race!
Carrying the baton for discourses
In politics, religion, economy and what nots:
Forcing us to bargain with our looks
And be bound to be misunderstood

Simply by the colours of our hoods!...
But underneath the skin, all is red flesh -
Nothing but red and white blood cells!
Under the skin, there are just bones-
Nothing but bones and more bones!
Under the skin, there are the veins-
Nothing but veins and billions of veins!

Under the skin there are arteries-
Nothing but veins and arteries!....
Names of the bones are the same!
Names of the organs the same!
Names of the fluids the same

The white and red cells look the same! - -
All degenerate and regenerate -
All consummate the human race!

During the trial of George Floyd's murderer, all the witnesses, both black and white of the different medical and non-medical professions, clearly testified to the *validity* of the fact stated above with their scientifically based and proven illustrations which therefore clearly indicts all those who are in the habit of discriminating against people of other races! Do not once again brush aside the fact that in reality, there is no scientific or biological basis for this racial phobia!

What is naturally evident here, is that which is only of the *spiritually unacceptable* approval of the appropriateness of anyone acquiescing to the notion of the *superiority* of one human spirit above another, which is at the root of humanity's deviation from obeying and doing the Will of God in this respect! This attitude is largely responsible for the actions of the majority of *prejudiced* police officers and many other law enforcers and despotic rulers everywhere, especially in places where the political system favours one group against another! This invariably results in events like that which is a validation of the above by the group of the proud nation's law enforcement officers who murdered George Floyd on that fateful day!

Our other big problem which *encourages* the perpetration of abominable acts as that of George's murder, or any other, is that we are *not aware* that our very own natural environments that operate in strict loyalty to the laws of existence, (while we don't) *react favourably or unfavourably* to all what we do daily!

Consequently, the enveloping atmosphere of the earth is now very heavily beclouded: polluted not only physically with all our industrial emissions but more so with our spiritual emissions of the dark energy radiations from all the atrocities we *daily* commit; including our evil and deviant thoughts, words and deeds!

Rest assured that the degree of cruelty and lovelessness of that abhorrent actions of the law enforcers who killed George Floyd in particular, in addition to the atrocities of the most recent deadly assaults on the lives of a certain cluster of cities in a European independent nation, will *certainly* trigger up and *add* to all of the accrued *repercussive* reactions of our *environmental partner* of existence!

This *adverse physical and spiritual condition*, is symptomatic of the extent to which cosmic equilibrium has been badly affected; leading to the increase of both spiritual and atmospheric *agitations*, released in the form of increasing psychically coded precipitations of all types of natural catastrophes! The global disasterous increase is a sure reflexion of the *hiatus* wreaked between mankind and nature in our continued blatant, egotistic noncompliance to God's laws! We should always bear in mind that we and nature have a symbiotic existence; one therefore reacts to what the other does always!

It therefore behoves us to strictly do only what accords with the natural laws of existence which are governed by *Divine Love* at all times! When we don't, the elements are bound to convulse and agitate in some visible unpleasant form to relieve themselves of the disharmonious and unexpected aberrant intrusions and negligence or deviations from the modus operandi of Creation's mechanisms, all of which are structured to ascertain that no other energy but that of Divine Love rules the universe! When this is obstructed in any corner of our world, chaos, decadence and degeneration loom over the life of man as is now evident!

Take the tragic and much feared and talked about "*Climate Change*" and the strings of disasters that it is unleashing on all of us! Judging by what has been said above, this phenomenon is taking place expectedly: because the original plan of doing things that are in accord with the Primordial Natural Laws of Creation, instituted by the Creator have *not* been maintained!

Paramount in these laws as repeatedly said, is that we should love others as we *love* ourselves under all circumstances! Since we don't, as was duly displayed by the murderers of George Floyd and many others round the world, nature which is suffused with love, is reacting in all the frightening ways we are seeing in all the present day countries of the world, thus confirming our alienation from the expected *universal norm!*

To live in harmony with man and nature, which is necessary for the purpose of our existence, we are required to do what nature does, i.e. comply with God's Laws! But under the siege of the blind callousness, power, greed and self-pride that have defiantly seized the human spirit's consciousness, and made us totally lose sight of the main purpose of our said granted incarnating here on earth: we have totally *reversed* our natural aptitude for doing only that which is good; which is what our *spirit requires* for its fulfilling that purpose of maturing into full spiritual consciousness for which it came to earth! We have instead reversed everything to that which will completely prevent us from *attaining* that purpose! Egged on by our over- developed and sagacious calculating intellect, we have thus typically gone from our previous natural *loving* state of existence, which would have prevented all atrocities like that which was committed against George Floyd and others, all the wars and prejudices and other deviations from observing the laws of existence as deigned by our Creator, and chosen rather to go from naturally being-

Colour blind in our childhood-
To colour phobia!`
Nationality blind in our childhood-
To xenophobia!
Status blind in our childhood –
To status hunting!
Clan blind in our childhood -
To tribalism!
Selflessness in our childhood -
To selfishness!
Image blindness - to vanity!
Religion blindness to spiritual banditry!
Political blindness- to ideological masturbation!
Race blindness- to crass racism!
Caste or clan blindness -to tribalism
Pride blindness -to narcissism!
Power blindness -to megalomania!

Hatred blindness -to war mongering!

Anger blindness -to irritability!
Envy blindness -to jealousy!
Cruelty blindness -to war and insensitivity!
We point fingers at each other and gesticulate,
Shaking our heads as we pontificate!
Railing over this, that and the other;
Not blaming selves but only others!
Crowding our days with crucibles of doom –
Reaching out for sympathy in our gloom!

Painting black white or camouflage,
Whichever will raise the flag,
Even if we die in the lies!
Changing camps at will in the sly.
Instead of the real us
That should only act with love,
Our demonised egos have become vain,
Making others writhe in mortal pain,
While we bask in pleasure and fame!

Instead of the real us
That should act with Love,
Our distorted egos discriminate!
Creating false images of selves.
Claiming rights denied others!
Instead of the real us
That should help all,
Our distorted egos ignore all;
Cramping Love in a cage of thorns!

Uwa Udensi Hunwick

Instead of the real us
That should act with grace,
Our distorted egos hatch disgrace,
Mindless of the shame we trail;
Leaving prudence in the lurch,
Smearing dung on the face of Love!
Instead of the real us
That should always be content,
Our distorted egos now salivate with greed!

Acquiring much more than we ever need,
Hoarding and cluttering our homes with goods
Most of which do no good!
Devising means to accumulate more,
Looting resources from many shores.
Spending millions to "fly to the moon"
While others rot in gloom!...
In place of the real us
That should shun high-horse rides,

We hunt for pomp and glory
And shun donkey riding in Christlike humility!
In place of the real us
That should only act with Love,
Our distorted egos have become prejudiced!
Fanning discontent, breeding vagrants
Upsetting the law of nature's equity!
Instead of the real us
That should always speak the truth,

Our distorted egos shamelessly lie!
Confusing man and nature,
Damning his own fate,
Devaluing his likeness of the Image of God!
Plotting his spiritual demise!
Instead of the real us
That should share the goods,
Nepotism reigns in all neighbourhoods,
Transforming us into cackling hens
Nesting only our family chicks –

Pecking at those that don't belong
To the coop secured by family bonds
Or sworn to the oaths of fraternity songs.
Instead of the real us
That should only espouse peace,
Our distorted egos take to violence,
With the patronage of hate;
Giving way to wild emotions
Coursing through us in wild confusion,

Making us lose the will to solve
All our ills with Love!
But in power lust,
Crack the whip of oppression,
Propping our cruel dispositions
With dominating intentions.
Keeping Love suspended
From our daily expressions - -
Gagging our spirits!

In our lives today, ask yourself why it is that you and I fail to heed the cries of people in grief, in the same manner that Derek Chauvin refused to heed the dying man's pleas for breath! Fail to look at the glaring grins of homeless men, women and children that line the streets, with pain and sorrow that has chiseled their frozen faces, labelling them abandoned; branding them as the forbidden and forgotten members of the human race, yet living in lands of milk and honey and the abundant gifts of nature! Not forgetting the plight of the suffering labour forces who are given the crumbs while their privileged employers gorge, which makes people like George Floyd unable to pay for his purported incriminating transaction! Why else do we do these things if not because we have simply *buried* our inherent true *spiritual* nature of beings suffused with particles of the benevolent power of the *Love* essence of our Creator, which we should daily apply for up-building, peace and happiness of everyone in our every day interactions with one another: but have become so *spiritually* obtuse as to be able to do what Derek Chauvin did to George!

Our civic, legal, social, educational, cultural and all the other institutions are all *compromised* in this, with biases for what alienates us from our desired spiritual goal! Replacing it with the insensitive orientation towards materiality only, which will invariably lead us to perdition! This state of affairs, is the reason that there is so much of inhumanity of man to his fellow man, which is diametrically opposed to the peace and joy that acts of *Unconditional Love* to one another evokes.

It is our *spiritually* required responsibility to employ all forms of unconditional love in whatever office we may hold, with whatever talent we may possess and whatever service we give to our fellowmen! Doing so will guarantee our full spiritual maturity in the earth *spiritual* school that we all are!

Covid 19 And George Floyd

All the undertakings of mankind which have all hitherto gone against the express will of God, are orchestrated by the sagacity of our overdeveloped intellect, which debars us from heeding the guidance of the small voice of the *intuition* out of the sola-plexus (our guts), by it's *suppression* of the input of the spiritual back brain and thereby dwindling its size!.....It is our duty to *reverse* this if we want to fulfil the said purpose of our incarnation on this earth! Here again George Floyd's life comes into view with regards to the purpose of his said "Mission Karma"

That mission *spiritually* prompts us not to so eagerly advocate our speedy return to the wrongly conceived "*normal*" ways of doing things, in the presumed aftermath of the Covid-19; without taking into consideration the *spiritual* significance and consequences of all that has been transpiring in our societies, that are in direct opposition to the said laws of Creation, which we *have not obeyed!*; The dangerous repercussions from this hubris on humanity's part is what , George Floyd is urging us all to avoid; through the resuscitating "*shocking*" effect of his murder!

Another major consideration is the fact that one thing always leads to another in the mechanism of the operation of Creation. That which leads is the spirit; , signifying that *everything is spiritually originated* and *then physically* manifested in their particular humanly recognisable characteristics This simply means that nothing happens in all of Creation without a valid spiritual blueprint!... The Corona virus took form therefore as a result of mankind's injection of various kinds of *defective* spiritual blueprints of "*life destructive*" acts of various magnitudes, into the creative mechanism of Creation, which prompted the spiritually created product of the same characteristics !

The aforementioned spiritual book "In The Light of Truth- The Grail Message", which is about Creation and man, reveals the fact that everything we do takes on its duplicate symbolic form, in the immediate physical world for us to harvest as pleasant earned rewards, or as what is wrongly considered to be punishments; symbolised by its duplicated ethereal counterpart, Divinely directed to come back to us for redemptive purposes, out of the Love of our Creator!

Over *centuries* of disobedience on our part of the Creator's adamantine commands, for which we have suffered many corrective or redemptive severe repercussions of various kinds, in form of plagues, natural disasters and what have you, without success; our continued injection of *more* spiritually inhibiting and "*life" destructive*" acts of different kinds, in direct opposition to God's All-Holy Will; have once again taken the repercussive ethereally replicated symbolic form of gradually but ultimately "*destroying*" our lives reciprocally: by slowly incapacitating the oxygenation of our bodies! Just as we have been gradually also incapacitating and destroying "our own spirits"!

Nothing ever comes from nothing in Creation. Thus our *loveless* lifestyles is systematically *stifling* our spiritual abilities which are the most important gifts for the *sustenance* of life itself! We are therefore *reaping* what we have been sowing for centuries in this pandemic again, and should not hastily return to doing all those *loveless* things which are antithetic to the *maintenance* of life in a universal atmosphere of peace and happiness, born out of loving one another, the absence or paucity of which is the bane of all societies of the world!

The Corona-virus created by us, has come back as another corrective force, buttressing George Floyd's mission to try to awaken us to reassess how we have stood in Creation so far. It is for all of us to come to know that we have been obstinately supplanting God's All-Holy Will of Love with our own, in the tragic greedy pursuit of all that is loveless and material only! This is clearly demonstrated in our burning bid to return to what we term "*normal life*", which is a misnomer for "*abnormal life*," of doing the following:

Trumpeting our bloated egos
With the wimpy wits

Of birds with broken wings
Propping our pride with the spoils of greed,
Washing our linens seemingly clean.
By cremating our consciences
At the alter of deceit,

The sepulchre of conceit,
The cathedral of opulence,
And the armoury of defences -
In the jungle policy of might is right!
Dismantling natural and societal norms,
Wheeling and dealing,
Stealing and peacocking,

Contracting backhanded deals.
Exploiting the have nots!...
We have no qualms about doing wrong,
Neither do we of what makes people frown.
We insinuate to implicate others,
Misinform to complicate matters,
Fake our wares to rake in more money!

We seem not to worry
So long as we swell our shares,
Leaving our consciences marooned and bare!
Exploiting our senses of mock superiority
To insulate our insecurity!...
While others gather crumbs from sties,
We garnish our breads with honey and spice!

Posturing futures secured in heaven
By the amount of money we have given

As tolls for our highways to heaven!
Sidetracking all the cardinal rules;
One of which is we should not lie.
But everyone lies
From morning till night!
The husband lies,
The wife lies,
The children lie,
The friend lies,
The enemy lies,
The master lies,
The servant lies!

The company lies,
The employee lies,
The banks lie,
The manufacturers lie,
The industrialists lie,
The policemen lie,
The lawyers lie!

Religious leaders lie,
Our rulers lie, -
All unworthy acts in God's sight!
The reaping of whose fruits
Can never escape Creation's rule !...
So write the love lestter
That nature dictates!

That is why the *loveless* defence, mounted by Derek Chauvin's group, failed but that of what represents unconditional and attested powers of love prevailed, and will always prevail in every case and happenings in Creation!

To our detriment, we let our better selves be fooled by champions of material progress, at the expense of the maintenance of our spiritual integrity, in the intellectually induced collective amnesia of all that makes us human!

Plunging us into uncontrollable broils from age to succeeding age, between man and man, one nation and another! This makes us want to reduce the psychic pressure this causes by jumping on to band wagons of anything that can assist in crowning us with worldly crowns, which however does not minimise our woes! So all around the world all we see in the spiritual fog — that surrounds us and is steadily choking us with our *approval* :—

Is the rabid grip of greedy guts,
Bloated with ill gotten golden stocks,
Smothering in vaults
Of xenophobia, and homophobia,
Of crass displays of biases,
Of all manias and phobias;
Dragging our future in the mud!

We grow financial greedy bugs
That ravage the have-nots
In their tattered huts !
Killing their virgin dreams,
Crippling their bids to compete
In sharing nature's feasts !...
Instead, we kill them!

We fail to dance
With our neighbours across the streets,
Across the boarder,
Homes, towns and villages.
Our workplaces fun places,
And our sporting places
Instead, we kill them!

Uwa Udensi Hunwick

Love is lost between one creed and the other,
One political group and another ,
One tribe and another,
One institution and another ,
One family and another -
In the collective amnesia
Of Living Love for ever!
Brewing her opposite in every land,
Precipitating the inevitability
Of man-made and natural disasters
That now relentlessly ravage all.
Rapping frantically at our consciences,
Nudging us to awaken from the nightmare;
So we don't kill but jilt:

The hegemony and superiority
Of one nation over another,
One tribe over another,
One clan over another ,
One class over another ,
One man over another ,
One gender over another!

Dislocating the natural order
With hubristic trust in our own powers,
While sinking in the sands -
Choking with blunt disdain
Of anything plain and sane
That does not spring
From our fevered brains!

Why George Floyd

We claim we have the ways with all
To make grass grow on frozen ice
With all that science can device!
We boast of having the means
To change the world to meet our needs -
Turning grass to gold
And earth to heaven ten-fold!

We know it all,
Can do it all,
In the paradise of fools
Who fail to employ the only tool
That can do it all—
LOVE—Living Love!
The Love with which we all are made!

The Social Cancer

As we witnessed in George Floyd's and Briana Taylor's cases and those of others before and since in many states across the nation of America, and of course all round the globe; we observe the following spiritually alienating habits that are prevalent in our societies today and even in the past, which are detrimental to our being able to achieve that which is our lives paramount goal: —

We slander,
A form of murder.
We cheat at whim
Even when we sleep.
We cheat our wives,
We cheat our husbands.
We cheat our friends...

We very often cheat the state;
Falsifying our pays every year!
We solicit falsely for donations,
Hire famous lawyers to defend our crimes -
Who twist the truth with legal jargons
That offer "alternative truths"!
In place of real truths!

We seize powers
And make the wise shudder!.
Do all abominable things with no bother,
Casting our fates

In reckless zest -
Head on to the brandishing blades
Of our karmic boomerang!

In doing all the above, we forget that God is Love and created all things out of that love with which alone we should operate in His Creation! In the process of creating man, did God discriminate for us to imitate Him as His children and aspirants of attaining the likenesses of His Image? Did He make some races fake, denying them what they need to succeed in their stipulated and *mandatory* spiritual quest. -

Then why do we do even worse by clamping down on people like George Floyd and all the deprived members of our shared world? By his manner of death, I am guided as before to say that George sought to make us change that and our other evil loveless ways, by subliminally prescribing the *review* of the culminating evil acts that factored into the happening of such an aberrant act as *that of his murder*, with the reminder that it has been quite.

Long we have played games
With our spiritual fate,
Betting on power not Love
To win the race.
Long we have punctured the sails
On boats that ferry those
Whose fortunes failed.

Long we have stolen
The rights of the meek.
Long we have broken
The backs of the weak,
Plundered their means
With equanimity and the bravado
Of the conquistadors!

Long has there been no end

To the jungle prima - facie elements
Of racial discrimination
In jobs and hiring places ,

Gyms, schools and fun places,
Education and housing places.
Health giving and funding places.
Discrimination against women persist,
Discrimination against gays persist,
Discrimination against lesbians persists,
Discrimination against races persist,
Discrimination against tribes persist ,
Discrimination against clans persists,
Discrimination against this or that persist!

Long have women lost their grace,
By coarsening their feminine traits,
Selling their spiritual privilege -
Their guardianship of the holy flame
For money and earthly fame!
Leaving the sheep without their shepherdess
To roam the world in pitch darkness!

Long have women wanted more clothes
To keep their self-esteem in place.
Long have women wanted more shoes
To give their styles some fancy boost.
Long have women wanted more jewelries,
To embellish other alluring fripperies
That catch salivating men!

Long have some wanted more coquetry:
With disks in their lips, ear lobes and tongue pins!
Long have women wanted more flatteries
To boost their lacking femininity!
Long have women lost their sense of shame
And their spiritual protective spells -
Making man shameless too!

Long also have men wanted more expensive cars
To exhibit their vain financial class!
Long have men wanted more women or male pals,
To satiate their overdriven carnal vibes!
Quite long have men wanted more money,
To fund their egotistic adventures
And their love for purse breaking sports!

Quite long have men wanted more power;
To dominate and subjugate others,
Validate their claim to honour
And advertise their brutal strength,
Boost their insatiable drive
To hustle and bustle -
Scrambling and trampling others down in the mix!

Men and women paying daily homage
To everything earthbound!...
We constitutionalise our misconceptions,
Indoctrinate with bigoted notions.
Formulate long formal protocols,
Coin up awe inspiring dogmas all
To cover up our systemic downfall!

These loveless drills with pungent innuendoes are the reasons the *whole* world has never yet come close to grappling with the unavoidable spiritual task that lie waiting for us now to undertaken for our eternal survival as executors of God's All- Holy Will, in the spiritually developing world. All that we have been achieving so far are so insignificant and transient as are evidenced in the demise of all the ancient civilisations cited earlier.

Archeological and oceanographic evidences exist that prove that our most advanced inventions say in aerodynamics, engineering, architecture and what have you, had been far surpassed by the inventors of the fallen old civilisations of Egypt, etc., including that of the sunken empire of Atlantis, to say the least.

Yet that empire and others after it *collapsed*, because of their lifestyles, which lacked the needed consistent maintenance of the pursuits of activities with true spiritual values, and aspirations!

At this Cosmic Turning point, every energy output of man in every aspect of his operations on earth is fusing to a crucible, which will *force* us all to either be spiritually awakened "*or*" *remain dead* and bound for extinction!

This force is being applied with the sword of Cleansing Light thrust into all of nature herself by the "*Son Of Man - Emanuel,*" the personified Holy Will of God, as revealed in the repeatedly mentioned spiritual book: so that the Divinely willed and spiritually well equipped man will finally emerge from his disintegrating material rubbles; to live in peace and joy as was Divinel planned!....

Because cosmic happenings *cannot change* to accommodate our continued intransigences, they are being compelled to enforce God's all Holy immutable Will on us, with *Love -* to foster our continued existence as part of nature; because *she cannot harbour* nor accommodate inhabitants that consistently only operate in manners that are alien to her spiritually well controlled ways of operation as willed by God! We have to cooperate and willingly synchronise with her loving intensions, to successfully restore the joyful effect of our endowed Life Giving power of Love!

Notably, the *beginnings* of the remedial flow of the power of love was induced to do just that to some extent that day when the whole world recognised the startling *lack* of love in the behaviours of the police officers who apprehended George Floyd and finally choked him to death that horrendous day!

It clearly demonstrated the uplifting *affect* of loving acts of any kind on the human psyche, much needed at this crucial "End Time". when auspiciously before his reincarnation, a *spirit* cared so much for the defaulting, spiritually non-responsive souls of his co-bungling fellow spirits, from life time to the other on earth; that in planning his contribution this time around, for helping us all awaken to our responsibilities as human spirits, who have continued to fail to achieve our said spiritual maturity; for which we have been reincarnating over and over again from the beginning of times: that human spirit called George Floyd decided to die a horrible death on earth to shock us back to pursuing that only quest for which we came to earth, before it is too late!

The reason behind that act of his, is one that all mankind should clearly cherish as an invaluable reminder of the one *spiritual* responsibility we cannot continue to evade! Which, if I may be permitted to reiterate is - doing all we can in the *consistent* application of the Sublime Love inherent in us in doing everything we do from day to day, which will not fail to lead us to attaining our indispensable spiritual maturity! Because in the unrelenting mechanism of the said Natural Law of Reciprocal Action, our acts of *unconditionally* loving others, by giving selfless services to our fellowmen, will help us reap acts of the same kind; which will make our world a happy place! Will certainly make us acceptable participants in the spiritual adventures of existence and gifted beings carrying out our expected development into the embodiment of the "likenesses of the Image of God", who are living with the burning desire to overcome any *militating* manmade spiritual drawbacks from the stipulated right track!

When this spiritual aspiration is *thwarted* or interfered with in any way whatsoever, as it has been the case in the lives of millions of the human spirits in the *prejudicial* systems of our nations; brought about and implemented either for sheer selfish, political, racial or religious reasons, or any of the obsessions of mankind from time immemorial, including the lust for *sheer power* by single individuals, societal classes, organisations or rulers and

Uwa Udensi Hunwick

demagogues of the world and recently by that which is transpiring in Ukraine: things go drastically wrong for everyone! These spiritual aberrations will unfailingly *militate* against the fulfilment of the very much needed achievement of the spiritual maturity of all in so many different ways, which often:

Drives man in desperation,
To raise the flag of consternation,
Destabilising his psychic equilibrium.
Dragging him down the street of disillusion,

To loose commitment to reality,
To humanity and society ,
To sincerity and loyalty,
To Civility and cordiality,
To Integrity and morality!

To non commitment to decency,
To truth and honesty ,
Transparency and clemency ,
Non-commitment to peace;
Non-commitment to compassion ,
Non-commitment to Love!

Non-commitment even to self
Non-commitment to life!
Non-commitment to anything!
But commitment to destruction,
Drug addiction and propagation,
Violence and hopelessness,
Facelessness and homelessness.

Playing into the jaws of rejection,

Even perhaps incarceration!
Disadvantaged and disgraced,
Demoralised
Dehumanised and dispirited!

Magnifying the fearful marks we make
On the sands of time -
With haunting scenes of -suicides,
Fratricides, homicides and matricides;
And recurring genocides...
Creating a disgruntled fake humanity,
In the style of disembodied demigods
Cocooned in an "insensitive"time capsule—
Facing the future it failed to foresee! —

Because it closed its eyes
To all the looming signs
That point to the Light!
The shinning Light
So bright
And so strong -
It quells all storms,
Diffuses all manmade bombs ;—
With its Unconditional Love to all!

The Selective Game

All the world governing bodies imagine that they can possibly *circumvent* the love mechanism of Creation by substituting it with their earthly manmade and intellectually derived laws and security devices. Both which are meant to prevent crimes and protect humanity with all manner of mechanical gadgets and invasive dangerous procedures that encroach on human health and rights, such as even scanning and implanting detective devices into the human body! An effort that is meant to ameliorate the prevailing chaotic conditions arising from our total divergence from depending on the spiritual laws which would have *definitely* protected us from any dangers internally and externally!

Yet these measures have not stemmed the world's financial instability, aggression, immorality, religious and political banditry; other related exploits of oppressive nature, nor have they curbed the prejudices that have only divided mankind rather than unite us; in the ensued castration of our true humanity in so many ways! For instance, it is rumoured, that there is even a plan afoot, of the threat of only breeding geniuses in the tuture, by scientifically engineered *selective* embryonic artificial conducted in labs! Above all, we continue to be each other's enemy rather than being " our brothers keepers ", and our intellectual agility is now further driving us to the escalation of confounding hair-raising hackings, and cyber attacks that are posing the grave danger of exploding the rampage of all that is evil and deterrent to our achieving the said only purpose of our existence on this earth!

All the above human attempts of replacing the only true and effective power for all our activities on earth, with manmade devises; only goes to increase the *danger* of our continued dependency on *mechanical* rather than our *spiritual* empathic means of securing personal and global peace and harmony: This visibly showcases the fatal spiritual price that is staring us all in the face especially at this "End Time" both as individuals as well as nations!

This scary situation and many others is why a caring and conscientious human spirit such as George Floyd chose to help in his own way. He was reminding us among other things, that our blind obsessions with material only accomplishments and power, is what has led to our:

Replacing Justice for all,
With justice for some.
Freedom for all,
With freedom for some.
Opportunities for all,
With opportunities for some.
Success for all,
With success for some!

Kindness to all,
With kindness to some.
Happiness for all,
With happiness for some.
Wealth for all,
With wealth for some.
Good health for all,
With that for some!

Good education for all,
With only for some.
Good social services for all,-
With just for some.
Peace for all,
With peace for some!
Happiness for all,
With sorrow for some!
Brotherliness for all,

With enmity for some!
Empathy for all,
Apathy for some.
Compassion for all,
With indifference for some.
Raising some up
Bringing some down,

Stepping on some to rise to the top,
Rather than raising them up to the top.
Sharing the wealth with everyone,
Rather than cutting some out!
Treating some with kindness,
Others with wickedness!
Loving some, hating some.
Feeding some, starving some.

Promoting parochial agendas,
Self centred agendas,
Image promoting agendas,
Power promoting agendas,
Hate instilling agendas,
Aggrandising agendas,
All forms of divisive agendas,
Rather than Loving agendas for all!

Now, wherever mankind looks there is despair instead of inspiring hope. Wherever we go there is fear and suspicion instead of joy in peoples' hearts! At every turn of the road there is despondency and apprehension by the underdogs of the society, who are afraid of being accused of having done something wrong simply because they look different or sound different or do things in unfamiliar ways!

This prejudicial treatment destroys our self confidence and reduces some to servitude, others to the acceptance of their degradation and helplessness, which in turn breeds and amplifies the desperate and rebellious acts which are now escalating round the globe! Coups, and other forms of insurrections, including homicidal activities abound to prove the point! *Monumental* demonstrations at a global scale of the event of George Floyd's murder, goes even further to hit the nail on its head, for all to see and make the necessary change that concerns all *insensitive* mankind in every field of life!

This is of the utmost importance for us as human spirits because, any human being who degrades the life and worth of another in one way or another, commits a violation of one of Creation's strict governing laws and will not fail to receive a fitting severe and due repercussive effect of the act in this life, or in the hereafter, in the operation of the Law of Reciprocal Action— "What you sow you must surely reap"!

Because the degradation of any life, let alone that of any human being, which automatically deflects one of Creations inviolable natural laws of existence, invariably cripples and hinders the true and overall physical and spiritual development of the victims of such treatments, who are consequently reduced to sadly living their entire lives with:

Fear haunting at the old and the young,
Treading gingerly on the paths of the fawns
Of traders of "power" for progress,
"Oppression" for freedom
And addiction
To vanity and insensitivity!

Flagging the illusion of liberation
Sautéed in psychic confusion -
In the fog of might is right!
Right is wrong!
Up is down -
In legal terms and legal facts

That negate the benefits
Of Living Love!

Amnesia rides the horse
Of who we are
And what to do
As likenesses of the Image of God!
And blurred our sights
In this scrambled world
Of greed and make-belief
Now we plunge head-on
With bigoted views,
Intimidating the unfortunate masses,
Coerced to the addictive negation
Of unconditional truth
For "alternative truths"

Abbreviated truths,
Qualified truths,
Hybridised truths,
Legalised truths,
Castrated truths
Specialised truths,
Imaginary truths,
Anything but The Truth!

The cardinal attribute of those
Created in the likenesses of the Image of God!
Turning our world into a battle ground
Of bedazzled antelopes trampling each other down
Castigating and humiliating each other,
Plotting and degrading each other...

Why George Floyd

Painting black white
Or white black for a prize!

Cynicism is now the escape
Of the dejected populace:
The bamboozled gullible hungry folks,
In politics and religion
Fashion and nutrition, sports and games.
Loosing the grip, -
The umbilical grip
To the why and wherefore
Humans preen like peacocks
But like ostriches
Bury their heads in the sand!

WE HAVE LOST THE GRIP!

Deranged Humanity

Rather than support each other toward achieving our common spiritual goal for which we are all here to do in the "*spiritual school*", we have turned around to do exactly the opposite, which makes us open to earning the spiritual and material just penalties that such hubris invariably brings! George Floyd's own spiritual experiences in past lives, made him take up the heavy and commendable responsibility of the help that he selflessly offered to his fellowmen in his said " Mission Karma" : because by all the evidences staring us in the fac today, we cannot deny the fact that without a doubt, we have-certainly done those things which are in *direct opposition* to the notion of living with the sublime love that is freely provided, for creating the proverbial *heaven on earth* we came here to establish as matured human spirits! This is a heavy burden that humanity is still carrying on its shoulders! This is the reason why an act like that of George Floyd's was meant to remind us to do away with those acts that keep stopping us from fulfilling our divine task!

All we have achieved so far is the proliferation of mostly all that is the replication of the "*hell*" we create in the beyond for ourselves with our evil acts on earth *in the present*, with acts such as: forcing the lowly and poverty stricken members of our societies anywhere in the world, to be condemned to live by the skin of their teeth as he George did! Letting them wade through disastrous storms with little or no financial nor medical assistance, but expecting them to skip to the sky and jump over the moon on witches' brooms as it were. Many other spiritually unacceptable acts such as the afore-said oppression, dishonesty, hypocrisy, bigotry, greed, violence, etc., etc., abound which have unequivocally retarded our spiritual growth before and s doing so again, right now as we speak!

Being spiritually *blinded* therefore, we have become unable to detect this disastrous spiritual trend which we have brought upon ourselves with, our thoughts, our words, and actions; because our materially fake, hypocrical and repressive lifestyles continue to prevent us from doing so. For example, we continue to —

Stab each other in the back,
And justify our acts
As tit for tat!
Or lick the boss's swollen boots,
Greasing his sweaty hands too,
Accepting the unacceptable,
Doing the unthinkable, -

To gain any amount of grounds
With those who wear the crown
And sit on thrones with royal frowns!
We turn blind eyes to vices,
To climb the ladders in guises,
Spread thorns on paths of others
But cover ours with fragrant flowers!.

It has become me, me, me and mine.-
I must have the best from the mines
To satisfy my self-pride.
The best cars
With golden bars,
The best suits,
The best shoes,

The best purses,
The best horses,
The best taste for anything, -
Women, men, friends and mates
And of course sex!

The best of life with all it takes;
In short, the best the world can offer

Without a thought for the other....
The hoarding against corona virus
Still fresh,
Who can forget?
Greed igniting crippling fevers,
Forging yet other deadly sins
That keep us spiritually limp!—

Making us continue to fail ourselves in this life's mission, by indulging in frivolity and the *debasement* of our spiritual integrity by deceiving and manipulating others at anytime; like at our private and public ceremonial events, which are calculated to leave a favourable impression on the minds of the attendees, who may be members of one political party or another, co-workers or business affiliates, friends, including bosses or just our admirers.etc.,etc.! —

So at these circuses of merry pretenders,
We raise our glasses with mixed agendas,
And toast accomplices with clenched fists:
Spreading conspiratorial grins
On faces flushed with jin!
Mocking our likenesses of God's Image,
In our depraved games!

Sometimes we adopt the look of regret,
So we may seem blessed
Yet as Judas Iscariot,
We betray humanity with avarice
Supplemented with embedded calumny,
Orchestrated in egomaniacal conspiracy,
Engineered by the pharisaical rich!

Why George Floyd

In our political theatres and cliques,
We humiliate others with our looks.
Subjugate them to insignificance,
Binding them in straight jackets
Volunteered by the cronies in our pockets-
All against our true nature -
As likenesses of the Image of the Creator!

What sad images have we been presenting to our Creator, Who has numerous times in the past sent us prophets, and other knowing ones and above all His own Son Jesus Christ, the real personification of Divine Love Himself; to redirect us towards pursuing lives of Love that are founded on high spiritual principles based on His teachings - but to no avail!

The fact that we have rather chosen to commit collective unthinkable spiritual suicide, by our unrelenting efforts to continue to retard our spiritual abilities, meant to enable us progress in the only direction that will lead us unfailingly to achieving our only reason for incarnating on this earth specially prepared for us: can undeniably be said to be the only reason why any human spirit would undertake to reincarnate on a "Mission Karma" of George Floyd's nature!

It being an emergency effort to rescue his fellow men from finally falling headlong into the pit of *self imposed* eternal damnation! He chose to do this as stated before to jolt mankind back to the recognition of our wrong doings in *not loving others as we love ourselves.*

A law that is paramount in Creation, because it is the essence of existence inherent in God Who is Love and the source of all life! Nothing else will work!

That is why it is said that *Sublime*, not *sensual* Love conquers all!

More Causes of Spiritual Retardation

At this stage of our *material only* advancement with little or no spiritual reservations or considerations, but agog and enchanted by our mind bungling but wrongly perceived material progress; we are literarily *swamped* with all manners of gadgets and apps for the immediate and speedy dissemination of information round the world, which like all other inventions of mankind, were meant to aid us in the furtherance of our *spiritual* growth, but have always been so *manipulated* by the *overdeveloped* intellect for material purpose, that they have become mostly used for destruction, like the nuclear energy turned into nuclear bombs and other things of destructive nature! All these retard our progress with the *spiritually* designed modules by which we are to operate! We continue to *sheepishly* adopt misleading *physical* only ways to function on a daily basis, not unexpected of the caricatures of our true selves that we have now become!

For instance, we spend endless hours watching *sensational, depraved and morally destructive and corrupting* programs and movies on the screens of the television or the cinemas! We spend equally endless time and money on the social media's gossiping fads such as proliferate in the internet namely: the twitter, facebook, instagram, tic-tock, and others; which most times spread falsehoods and destructive rather than upbuilding rumours at a blink of an eye! All increasingly jeopardising our *resistance* to the already harmful existential debilitating and retarding spiritual *fog* which is now suffocating all mankind!

As individuals we continuously contribute to this retarding worldly preoccupation which we apparently do not consider harmful, but in reality are a great deal so. That people like Derek Chauvin and others did and still do the terrible things they do, comes from the fact that we encourage them on a daily basis by toying with *thoughts* of harming or even killing someone which, though we do not actually carry out, nevertheless influence is magnetically attracted to and empower anyone who is so inclined anywhere in the world who then actualises our intents. In the mechanism of Creation, this automatically makes us *accomplices* in all the crimes and atrocities we all complain so much about, perpetrated by *those* others who however, we have unknowingly influenced!

Judging by this spiritual *reality*, we should be very concerned about, the likelihood that, we have in many different ways, *contributed* to the insensitivity and inhumanity that finally culminated in that murderous act of Derek Chauvin and others like him:, through the magnetic radiations of our thoughts, words, and actions; in the law of like attracting likes! Such sublime *empowerment* was originally meant to achieve the reverse! The Almighty wove this influencing mechanism into the workings of Creation for us to be able to *remotely and spiritually* help one another in achieving *all that is good only; in support of* that common spiritual goal for which He allowed us to incarnate in His magnificent Creation!

Our failure so far and indeed before now, in fulfilling that required sublime only goal, lies in our continued indulgence in the magnetic spiritual quagmire of different seriously entrapping misapplication of the gift of being able to *speak*, as one of the aforementioned three major abilities we possess with which to operate, but which we have turned into *self destructive* weapons in practice! For in stance, we have formed the habitual pastimes of lying rumour mongering, killing and so on, accompanied with the thought that gave them birth and the distasteful actions that follow suit. All these undermine and degrade the *sacred values and efficacy* of the said abilities in the promotion of our spiritual progress! For instance *words, as well as the other two abilities* are spiritually meant *strictly* for the ennoblement edification and upbuilding of the human spirit *only* and not for frivolous and destructive egotistic engagements of any kind, either at home, schools colleges, clubs or at work; where we invariably trespass in the following different instances such as when—

Men gossip,

Women gossip,

The old gossip,

The young gossip, -
Maligning each other,
Ridiculing each other,
Degrading each other,
Demeaning each other,
Defaming each other!

Demonising each other,
Dehumanising each other,
Destroying each other; -
Passing the dark art from one to the other
Mouth to mouth and media to media.
Perpetuating the danger
As the young copy us,
Cheating and stealing,
Copy us deceiving.

The young copy us swearing,
Copy us sneering,
Copy us doing
The things we shouldn't be doing!
Copy our moral laxity,
Copy our depravity,
Mimicking our ignominy
In yielding to infamy.
They copy our inconsistencies:

They repeat our prejudices and hypocrisies,
Our bigotry and frivolity,
Our insincerity.
They copy every step we take....

They have no choice but to replicate
The things we do in the same trail.
And cannot help but fall where we fell,
Trip where we tripped,
Drown in the cesspool of our ills!

Life for them is constant gravitation
From saintliness to sinfulness -
With jumbled emblems tattooed with ballads
From family pallets -
Clouding their visions with fumes
That characterise their family brews!
The child waxing strong in this brand,
Cannot fail to carve a matching boomerang
From the family heirloom.

Inciting him to lie and bully at school
Or fight and cheat a handful.-
In the law of like father like his brood.
Do all the things the parents do,
Sampling the fruits from the cabinet
Of the parental tutelage....
Peer pressure in constant collusion
With increasing delusion
Compel attention!

The youngster capitulates,
With burning intention
To one or the other in equal proportion.
The teenager steps out with the desire
To set the world on fire!

With the tentacles of an octopus
And the will of a Vesuvius,
Spewing its characteristic lava:
Ravaging the world with inconceivable caviars

Of compounded hot recipes;
Declaring his ideologies.
Blazing the trail with passion and visions.
Painting the world with projection
Of apocalyptic proportions!....
At colleges the broths of acculturation thicken,
The scope of intellection broadens,
The power of indoctrination strengthens;
Sororities and fraternities accentuate,

Duplicate and sublimate,
Consecrating and sanctifying peculiar notions
Of what is fact and what is fiction.
Formulating outlandish ideologies
That typify their insecurities,
In the challenging taste of realities
Branded by shattered humanity
Staggering with instability,
Suppurating with insincerity,

Hardened with insensitivity.
Debased with hypocrisy,
Unreliable with inconsistency,
Intolerant with bigotry,
Immoral with carnality and sensuality!...
Beleaguered by greed induced strifes,

Jaundiced with phobias and racial strifes,
Deformed by intolerance on the rise;
In the miuse of the three spiritual rights!

The spiritual retardation further continues in everything the youth does, be it in sports and other social engagements. Greed courting greed, phobia espousing phobias, racism promoting racism, discrimination sponsoring bigotry and other *spiritual* retarding attitudes, in fraternities and student organisations; in the law of like *attracting likes*. And the struggle between doing what is good and what is evil escalates! Thus after graduation, the bewildered youth goes into the bewildered world only to replicate the father while the daughter replicates the mother. The initiate replicating the mentor who in spiritual evaluation at this crucial time is equivalent to *the blind leading the blinded!* ....

This has gone on from one generation to the next and from one ancestry to the next to the extent that, in the effort to free his or herself from all ensuing earthly pressures, the fledgling young spirits *copy* the adults in letting all spiritual principles give way to *expediency*; where favours are sought exacted or demanded! Hands washing other dirty hands, abandoning all constraint without resistance, lest he or she is wrongly deemed *unprogressive* Shunning morality with the deceit of misapplied freedom of expression in the *spiritually* crippling *mud* of intellectual "modernism"! With time tested edicts on the modern chopping boards, the youths join the club of *lost* heroes in the bungled fight for our spiritual survival !

But people like George Floyd have intervened with the hope of helping us beat all bad habits and retrieve our humanity y, by the revival of the good habit of utilising our precious spiritual abilities of thoughts, words and deed of *Sublime Unconditional Love!*

Terrifying Impacts of Our Disobedience

In addition to the strangle hold of these perversions having Spiritually *crippled* all humanity young and old, it has also finally plunged us headlong on the path of an increasing *monumental* corresponding karmic repercussions, from which we will find it very hard to escape, if we do not *learn* the spiritual lessons in the mission of George Floyd and the fearful scourge of the Covid 19!

His said attempt to *forestall* this foreseeable *destruction of all humanity,* which is the predicted repercussion culminating from all our aberrant behaviours; topped by our insistent and over-the-top "*self-centredness*," becomes clearly understandable! It is me, me, me and mine all the time, to the exclusion of all others!

On the other hand, the desire not to ever do anything that will harm or go against one's own interest is a natural instinct for self preservation, which practically governs all that mankind does. This natural instinct however, is also meant for us to apply in all our dealings with one another as we pursue our spiritual and material development and therefore should never be denied or wrenched from anyone; but should rather be the empathic means by which we conduct our relationships! In other words we should do unto *others as we would want done to us!*

But because of our perversions and "self-indulgent ambitions of various natures, the opposite sentiment of infringement on individual human rights has become the norm. George Floyd and others would be alive today if Derek Chauvin "did to him the way would have wanted it done to himself"!

At the national level, obsessive self interest has bred imperialism, colonialism and other forms of aggression, oppression and exploitations: putting other peoples' lives in danger, with grievous human rights abuses, as suppression succeeds discrimination, bigotry succeeds exclusion, deprivation succeeds prejudice, injustice succeeds intolerance and greed takes over from monopoly. Worst of all is the dehumanisation aspect which follows deprivation and character defamation, garnished with simmering streaks of jealousy. All these are climaxed by *hatred*, the antithesis of Love and a standard measure of a system that champions pride and superiority complexes and the power of heritage and privilege; which drive the claimants to subjugate anyone of choice, into living subservient unproductive lives!

The type of life that led George Floyd and others in this lifetime to be treated the way he was treated, and which he had wanted to expose in his "Mission Karma" in order that we would reject it and return to the original all *inclusive* Divine plan, in which all humanity are to collaborate with each other in making inspiring contributions with their talents, necessary for the overall success of everyone in the achievement of our common spiritual maturity on Earth.--!

All hands were and are still to be on deck as nature dictates:

For if all the trees were oak,
All the palms the nut-coco,
All the bushes nettles,
All the weeds thistles,
All the animals apes,
All the fishes whales,
All the reptiles cobras,
All the seasons winter,
All the insects mosquitoes,
All the food Dorito's,
All lands deserts,
All fruits banana,
All the meals akara,
All sounds one-note,
All the meat beef,
All vegetable collard green;

All drinks Jin,
All songs hymns,
All humans the same:
All males
Or all females, -

Dressed the same way,
Spoke the same way,
And ate the same food everyday...
What a strange world that would be!—

Why then do we *scheme* against *racial* diversity which validates racial equality and justifies social equity, so that we can express our inspiring individualities with *unbiased Love*, preventing the perpetration of the hatred of one man and another just because of the differences in skin colours languages cultural or social backgrounds or religions?!

The dastardly murder in his "Mission Karma" of which the entire world disapproved, lends credence to the fact that George Floyd *seriously* meant to leave the following spiritual, pertinent personal questions to everyone of us, who dream of achieving the goal of our repeated sojourning on earth. Bearing in mind that we are all only still here today because: we have *not been* able to attain our spiritual "*graduation*" so to say; but have obviously been *continuously failing* and therefore been reincarnating for repeated atonements for our pervious sins and the necessary reorientation to doing only what will afford us the required *spiritual* maturity!

So by his gruesome murder he impressed upon our minds the evils we must all always strive to avoid! He evoked the following indisputable facts which should rouse all mankind to always remember those cardinal spiritual taboos, paramount to our achieving that all important spiritual goal! These refer to the fact that intuitively, no one wants to be hated, nor his or her life be degraded, simply because he or she looks different, or does things differently! Above all no one likes to be killed! No one wants to be stereotyped nor be racially or socially profiled, ridiculed or abused and jailed for little or no reason, let alone be tortured and finally murdered! He lets us remember that in so doing, we would again not be doing to our fellowmen the way we would want done to us!

George Floyd in his choice of death also demonstrated the factual inhumanity of being dispossessed of human dignity and the *right* to live, which no one should take away from anyone, but which we continue to do, asking: Have we done to them as we would want it done to us?

Would Derek Chauvin and his mates want what they did to George be done to them? Definitely no!

The Bane of Slavery

The evil outcome of slavery in all guises in ancient and modern times, stares everyone starkly in the face, because it is at the root of all the atrocities of man's inhumanity to his fellow man! Calling to mind the lynching, the burning, the executions, rapes, mutilations, castrations and so on, which in their wake have spiritually burdened all those who imagine they have benefitted from their exploits round the globe!

Enslavement of any human spirit represents a clear insult to the Creator of the universe, Whose right to the ownership of all life cannot be appropriated by the creature He Himself created; all of whom He gave the same *irreversible* spiritual qualities and abilities for the fulfilment *of the same spiritual goal!* -

The havoc that slavery has wreaked in the psyche and spiritual as well as material welfare of humanity everywhere in the world, cannot be over-emphasised nor overlooked; because of the devastating dehumanisation, deprivation and general obvious psychological destructive effects it has had on the *race* that has borne the brunt of the many evil *perpetrated* under its banner! It is definitely the origin of all what people like George Floyd and others of any race and demography, have had to go through in many life times; and undeniably the *underlying* factor that brought him to the world's civil and political frontline this time around; in his desperate bid to enable the most needed us restorrestoration of our lost spiritual abilities to live freely together as comrades in pursuit of the same spiritual goal!

George Floyd's spiritual struggles in many life times must have brought him to this point in his growth, in spite of all odds; which made him decide in this particular reincarnation, to take on the task of purposely *helping* his fellowmen *remember* who they are and *what they are meant to be doing here on earth*, no matter what!

Permit me to reiterate that it is *strictly* for us to attain that spiritual maturity, because we are spirits wearing the body with our smart intellect only as a tool which do not have any spiritual abilities whatsoever and yet on which we completely rely, which has led to its being overdeveloped, though its abilities are only temporal and manipulative; leading us to completely forget to commit to be committed to anything spiritual!...

It can dissect and analyse, calculate and project, invent and manipulate only earthly materials to whatever level we want; but it does not and cannot understand nor is it able to lead us to success in our spiritual *quest*! Its domain is strictly bound to materiality and can only remain so!

In all his and our reincarnated experiences in our said quest, George Floyd must have also learnt that our world so adulate and base all our interactions and accomplishments on all things derived from the rapacious and sagacious exploits of our *beloved* intellect, to the extent that we ever judge different human races *mostly* by their intellectual prowess and achievements; arising from the long cultivation of the wrong habit of evaluating everything with our intellect which can only recognise and propagate same on its limited physical level, to achieve what can be visibly seen and deemed outstanding, magnificent and ostentatiously grandiose!

In all these *self glorifying intellectual engagements*, we forget that all the world's past civilisations, with their ingenious edifice's of startling monumental proportions, which were intellectually conceived and executed even though commendabe admittedly innovative, ambitious and grandiose are only transient, commodities, which in spiritual reality; actually have no value for them nor for us, both of whose only purpose for existence is for the achievement of that which survives time and space and human machination for all eternity! Anything else we achieve physically is of but a secondary value in its being only of a material nature and can be said to be a waste of time energy and resources!

Yet our world continues to be controlled by self-centred, rich and materially oriented individuals and nations, who joke at prevailing vices and blink at our gravitation to obsessions that *swell* their purses, sanctioning moral laxities and infatuations which foil our spiritual purpose, in th *perverted illusion of progress!* This has continued to make mankind as a whole to turn away from all constraints of ethical norms in all our pursuits, no matter what it may be. For a glaring example, in the entertainment industry, *anything* goes; opening the gate to unlimited scopes of hair and brow raising moral and ethical throes: in the overthrow of the sacredness of life, decency and human integrity in their unfitting *decadent and violent* plots, dressed and glossily sold on the silver screens round the globe! All for the enrichment of the rich cliques who sponsor and produce them. Along with it is the exploitation again of the teaming labour force of men and women aspiring to make it in a competitive desolated world of "*dog eating dog*" as the saying goes! This industry more than any other, needs to redirect its very influential ability towards the propagation of events of high spiritual values that will enable us fulfil our said only purpose here on earth. Just like George Floyd wished to achieve in his "Mission Karmic" death! We all need to refocus our activities towards that also because we are   all in the same predicament!

Fashion designers, capitulating to greed and lust for fame, following suit in the degradation of our spiritual integrity by *stripping women* of shame, which further leads mankind to waywardness and departures from the laid down moral rules indicated in the commandments of God the Creator. And the world ruling systems continue to fall prey to manipulators, bigots, dictators and demagogues, sharpening their weapons of suppression and oppression; *subverting* the power of Divine unconditional sublime Love, but fanning the flames of hatred in all its guises!

We all naturally know, that *wealth* and power blur and often times simply blunt man's sense of appropriateness, even shutting down our feelings, reducing it to the horror of the insensitive level of instigating wars and now, the *stifling of sacred life* out of a fellow human being. This is comparable to the lynchings and the like that had gone on before. Such acts are not only regrettable but spiritually condemnable, as they can only lead us towards well deserved perdition; which was one of the overall reasons for the spiritual action George Floyd took: for right now, we are living in a virtual fool's paradise where- -

The greedy has become the economist,

The racist has become the nationalist,
The flirt has become the gallant;
The hypocrite the purveyor of truth-
And the servant of God!
The callous the prude,
The murderer the hero.
The ignoble the noble.
The anarchist the patriot.
The molester the chaste,
The lier the saint!
The megalomanic the champion.
The corrupter the saviour,
Making corruption a way to beat
Our vices with much ease.

All aspects of our lives are thus *corrupted* and have veered away from the expectations of the life styles of those eager to spiritually develop themselve to the likeness of God's Image as Divinely expected of them. This is eviden in the way we generally conduct our lives by the way we speak, the way w breed, the words we say, the way we relate as citizens, races, nationalities, co workers; in short by the way we treat each other anywhere and any time. W continue to intimidate and hurt one another, threatening and taking on another's very life, making us feel totally insecure everywhere; when we wer meant to live peaceably together as the result of sharing our love of on another. Instead everywhere and every time now, even as we speak, we are -

Insecure in our homes,
Insecure in our yards,
Insecure at the fair,
Insecure in our farms,
Our synagogues and mosques,
Or even having some fun!
Not safe at night

Even with lights.
Not safe in the village
Where there is much pillage
Not safe in the city

Where there is less pity.
We are confronted with wrongs
And are haunted with guns!
We are threatened with laws;
And are threatened with wars;
In a world that is lacking in Living Love,
And does not care for each other,
But fear each other,
And suspect each other,
Having failed
To let Love prevail!

Why George Floyd

Our Corrupted World

In the aftermath of George Floyd's murder, as conscientious discerning human spirits we cannot but inwardly see that the *fake piety* that we proffer in all guises has truly been to our greatest disadvantage. Because it has destroyed our chances of being able to wade thorough the meshes created by our hypocrisies and insincerity; which *collectively* have inevitably yielded their own corrupted versions of Love, devoid of all spiritual contents and considerations; as we saw on that fateful day of George Lloyd's murder!-......

The overall intention of this book is not only to make it known that George Floyd did not just die in a terrifying event of a "*Mission Karma*" in the hands of an agents of a supposedly law enforcement institution of "a nation under God", but also to make it clear that, what is of the most *spiritual* importance in this regard to all of us, is that we *reconsider* the parts we have played and continue to play in this *regularly* committed loveless acts that have culminated in the demonstration of a worldwide unanimous renunciation and condemnation! That act of Derek Chauvin and others like him through the ages clearly demonstrate the *absence* of the major spiritual quality of a human being of any nation, let alone that of one vowed to be "*under God*" Who is Love!

We need to do the reconsideration in order to effect the desired genuine *spiritually* motivated changes that are absolutely necessary for our own salvation. In other words, we should not continue to be *indifferent* to our own fate nor fight shy of end eavouring to truly understand how we as human spirits got to this devastating point, in our millions of years of developmental march towards spiritual enlightenment and fulfilment.

If we don't do this appraisal, all our outbursts and civil agitations will only be *ensconced* in the glorified archives of museums, and chronicled in history books just like the others before, and nothing significant will change

But we are all now being advised by Abd-ru-shin, the Bringer of "*In the Light of Truth- The Grail Message*", *to make that necessary* change in the looming emergency of the End Time!

What has been missing is the fact that no one has ever looked for the reason for this perpetual abnormal *non spiritualised* earthly human behaviour beyond rummaging through all what is *physical* only!

The reason for this oversight lies in the fact that we have been wrongly operating only with our overdeveloped intellect which is the less perceptive instrument for the cognition of anything beyond the physical as been stated! This has indeed impaired our ability to grasp or perceive what is outside its scope.

As stated earlier also, we possess both the now *larger* and overdeveloped intellectual frontal brain known as the cerebrum, for solving all that is physical and therefore temporal, and the now *shrunken smaller* back spiritual brain the cerebellum, for perceiving and solving what is spiritual. The over use of the former enabled it to grow larger and stronger, suppressing the latter and reducing it in size and participation in our decision making at any given time! The latter's prompting and superior *guiding* voice being reduced to a tiny whisper in our consciences which we most often ignore only to regret doing so later!

This little voice we constantly ignore, is our *intuitive* prompter, which is like a radar that *scans the universe* for spiritual solutions on any matter that concerns the human spirit in the pursuit of the fulfilment of our given purpose of existence as human spirits! It is located in our back brain whose shrunken size has incapacitated it and consequently forced us to loose the awareness that we are not what we were meant to be any more!

We now only understand a *tenth* of what is spiritual. The rest is lost to us! Clairvoyants and clairaudients and the like however, can sometimes receive spiritual impressions or pictures, whose interpretation are compromised by their being subject to intellectual interference! Young children are mostly able to keep the back brain unfettered with worldly matters, that's why they can remember past lives much more easily than adults with all the clutter of intellectual garbages we are so proud of. This cluttering and suppression of the spiritual brain is why we are not able to remember that we have been coming back to earth school many times before!

Some human spirits however are subconsciously aware of this natural occurrence and are able to take advantage of what it offers them for atonement of their karma. Others like George Floyd died the way they did in their subconscious awareness of this, by using the opportunity to help their fellowmen, in this case by wanting to jolt us back to the normalcy of remembering who we are and why we are here on this earth and therefore to pursue the only path that will lead us to that aforementioned only goal!

At a subconscious level, all of us must have invariably suffered many set-backs in many aspects of our lives, both in previous incarnations and now typically either because of our race or other prejudicial factors like class wealth or power, etc., and are therefore subliminally aware that our world is totally misled in understanding the power of Love which has been corrupted in many ways, especially in its bonding and peace generating abilities!

For example, in our *misunderstanding*, we have confined the expression of Love within our homes alone, adding sexual aggrandisement anywhere anytime with it, thereby stripping it of its spiritual power; associating i mainly with having *physical* pleasure and satisfaction once more!

We have also transformed its bonding abilities to galvanising communities for *selfish* purposes, where the ethnic majority dominates the population, under the selfish umbrella of self pride and ethnic preservation turning it into a weapon against those in minority where it can easily become a matter of life and death!

All these ways have lead us no where so far, neither would the prevailing defeatist attitude of *complacency*. On the contrary, it has additionally deflated humanity's spiritual aspirations and obliterated the necessity of sharing our sublime gift of *unconditional* Love, rendering us victims of despondency!

That's why we should embrace the *wake up call* of George Floyd and take immediate progressive spiritual action on our own behalf!

Having lived other lives before this as all of us have, whether we remember or even believe it or not, he had most likely seen the continued *danger* posed by our *self-complacency* and obstinacy in complying to Creation's rules which spiritually retard us, that he made the decision to then take on the "mission karma". As a rule in Creation, such is done only on behalf of others as stated earlier. At this particular time, it was necessary that we are persuaded to clearly see the extent of the *devastating* harm we have done to ourselves by again falling into the trap of our *power greed and self-centredness* in every sphere of our life pursuits! In this, no occupation, business, foundations, organisation or institution is exonerated! All have become blind to everything that work against our needed spiritual progress, one of which *corruption. - -*

Corruption of all types permeates all spheres of our human life, leading us to abandon all our inherent natural spiritual principles; eroding and obliterating our innate sense of what is right and what is not; leaving us to accept and endure our distorted lives, burdened with these unfortunate fact that:

Our politics is corrupted.

Our social life is corrupted.

Our social services are corrupted.

Our gender identity is corrupted.

The matrimonial institution is corrupted.

The health care institution is corrupted .

The agricultural system is corrupted.

The food supply chain is corrupted.

Our financial system is corrupted.

Our employment system is corrupted.

Our industries are corrupted.

Our amusements are corrupted.

Our religious systems are corrupted.-

So are their leaders!

Stamping out the discovery
Of the irrefutable natural facts of life,
Confusing spiritual and human rights,
Doping our inquisitive minds
In overt religious rites,
With palliative pills of castles in heaven.!
Turning religion into a vending haven
For fast redemptive leavens
That charm the doting devotees
Populating the putrid undergrounds
Of misguided humankind.-
In a world of make -belief
And mass spiritual -deceit
Of the weakened souls of humanity!

As a human spirit, you are subconsciously a seeker so long as you are constrained to be here on earth! This is a spiritually instilled or innate gift, to foster the impetus for the acquisition of requisite spiritual guidance for our survival on the material environment of the earth. It is that which makes us return to earth time and time again where we don't belong, to be able to finally resolve our recurrent karmic issues and become free of any further retributive occurrences in our lives now and in the future!

To be able to gain that freedom in the future is largely dependent on our responses to the selfless act of the Mission Karmic death of George Floyd in question, which would undeniably be to our detriment if we underplay or ignore its timely loving message, pertinent for humanity's continued survival in creation! But the said —

Corruption in religion,
Has fed adherents with jaundiced verses
That make them lose all common sense,
Turning some into fanatics
Of political or religious causes,

Civic or self-centred causes,
Racial or ethnic causes;
Magnifying the banes of intolerance,
Escalating the pungency
Of the moral morass,
And Faith morass,
The social chaos,
The political chaos,
That have defaced humanity!

It is obvious from the foregoing observations, that corruption in religion has greatly contributed to what has turned mankind away from the right way to function in the *All-Holy Will of God*, in a universally *love* controlled universe! With its manipulative doctrinal power, it overshot the spiritual parameters of its operations with intellectually conceived theological jargons and ceremonies of its own creation.

Consequently this among many other militating offences, has led us to becoming *totally* blocked from truly understanding how to operate in the world which is *spiritually* controlled from above!

God alone makes the rules!

The matrimonial institution is another sore example which drives the nail even deeper, because of the mainly material basis upon which the unions are made, which invariably falsifies their enactment, reducing the partners —

To junkies in the trade of the flesh!
Converts the candidates
To perpetual gamblers
Fated to inescapable escapades
Of emotional piracy,
Rapes, delusions and deceptions;
Sexual harassments and seductions.

Drags lives through labyrinths

Of intrigues that turn marriages
Into contracts bound by money.
Infidelity lurking in every closet,
Breaking down the matrimonial concept!
The man playing the masculine card with a rod :
Sucking up the union's free fresh blood,

Triggering off matrimonial blood clots
Clogging up the woman's sacred call!
For her's is not a bed-mate role!
Her's is not a door-mat role!
Her's is not a chattel role!
Neither is it a dominating role,
Nor is it a submissive role!

Her sensitivity gives strength to her tasks.
Her heightened intuition backs her stance-
So long as she keeps her priestess-hood
Of purity in womanhood in tact.
Her's is not to compete with her man,
Her's it is to lead her man's band,
And inspire the dreams he tills in the fields.

Her's is not to provide for the breeds,
Her's it is to ennoble the yields
Of all the matrimonial seeds.
The purity of her disposition sets her tone
As the guardian "priestess" of the home!...
But single parenthood has changed the rules.
Breeding delinquent Robin Hoods.

Natural balance now lost in the hoods,

Suicides and addictions haunt the grounds
Where insecurity breeds gangsters hounds.
Immorality in all guises abound,
Seeping through the rank and file
Of victims in their daily lives.
With molestations and rapes on the side,

Trafficking and kidnapping on the rise,
Harlotry and pimping in their trail.,
Daily life is daily hell!...
The child in this haunted sty,
Armed with one wing in this isle
Cannot fly high enough to hide
From the persistent piercing hang man's bells-

The sirens of the juvenile jails,
Built specifically for the abandoned ones
Of generations born,
In quest of the same spiritual dawn!
But who have fallen through the cracks
Created by all our acts
Of insensitivity and lack of Love!

Derek Chauvin's *callous* and *insensitive* behaviour is an example of the spiritually damaging effect of our living loveless and uncompassionate lives in one way or another, which jars and *distorts* our psyche: Resulting in acts and goals that are not in conformity with the normal expectation from a normal human spirit, but that borne out of the *misconceptions* of what life is all about, as he clearly demonstrated.

The second half of the poem is indicative of the typical scenarios in the daily lives in communities of the underprivileged and oppressed people everywhere including here in America, where George Floyd faced challenges comparable to what other typically deprived people undergo either in his then present lifetime or in previous incarnations here or elsewhere in the world. Such that in this life just brutally ended and which was reminiscent of past experiences, lent a hand in his spiritual decision before birth, to undertake the redeeming course of a Mission Karmic death for the benefit of every human spirit at this most critical point in our collective spiritual developmental journey!

At the same time, Derek Chauvin's callous behaviour also mirrors what has persisted throughout known human history and have proven that we are still living self imposed ignorant, spiritual suicidal lives, that have caused us to return time and time again to different parts of the world most suitable for us to effect the necessary changes that will reflect who we truly are and how we should proceed to live as spirits in need of spiritual development and nothing else! The impact of his committing that murderous act this time around; has served him and the world the purpose of discouraging the perpetration of future similar acts…. He will never do that again!

It is therefore absolutely necessary for us to understand and truly believe that for our continued existence as human spirits on this earth, which is governed by highly potent invisible spiritual Laws that supersede *manmade* *ones*, such as to which Derek Chauvin and his mates were adhering; we *must* desist from *ignoring* our spiritual development that is based on irreversible life preserving principles , which have little or nothing at all to do with attendances to sworn religious services and the touting of the names of Jesus and God or Buddha or Mohamed etc., in all the languages there are!: burying our heads in the proverbial sand, or worst still! in our delusional atheism while committing more abominable acts! Not realising that the very vigilant and active primordial natural laws of creation take reciprocal actions for or against any form of acts of infringements that may occur in any aspect of their checking and balancing operation, committed by anyone of us at any time and anywhere in all of Creation. All for our own good!

It is also for our own good that all the phenomenal and so called mysterious happenings that man did not manufacture round the world, such as the parting of the Red Sea in Biblical Egypt, the forty years deluge of Noah's time, etc., in Christian theology and many more in the phenomena evolution of man and the earth and all that exists, visible and invisible, including the galaxies and the ever expanding- universe itself: the differences in the seasons of the earth, the flora and the fauna, etc., etc., give testimonies of the powerful and watchful presence, domination and supremacy of the invisible sublime *spiritual power* over all that is physical! That this Primordial power is that of the Sublime Power of God the Father's *Love*, with which *He created and strictly runs everything*; stubborn *loveless* humanity has been playing with fire for a very long time now courting heavy retributive reaping of what we have been sowing!

Hence our only assured *providential* escape from the scheduled destruction at this End Time of the cosmically scheduled human spiritual maturity, lies only in our living a totally different life completely based on having *Unconditional Love;* in strict obedience to the will of God. Such alone will definitely prevent us from further commitments of acts like the ones that took George Floyd's life and those of others like, Briana Taylor and many others!

Also, the desire and obsession with what *money* can buy and the power we can derive from having it, which drives us to lie and do all the evil things we do, is the vicious multi-headed snake that needs to be expunged from our distorted individual and national psyche!

It is at the center of the *brewery* of all the evils that intoxicate us to the extent of *desensitising* us from caring to attain the said crucial spiritual maturity of all humanity! We truly *debar* ourselves from achieving that goal, with the attending reward of heavenly blessings in all we encounter, even though we live in the *delusion* that we can: because of the fallacy of a propitiatory sacrifice of the pure and innocent blood of Jesus, or of animals and so on; avoiding the irrevocable fact that we are *only* pilling up our own individual and national karmaic debts by doing so!

Political Corruption

Let us examine our political engines which are replete with moral and ethical flaws that make anyone engaged in the failed institution for the governance of a people, in all its notoriously distorted forms everywhere become suspect of harbouring some degree of egocentricity, which above all else leaves much room for *humility*- a paramount quality in a human spirit It is in politics that all forms of vices rear their ugly devouring heads o clannish, racist, phobic, and what have you sentiments! These always devolve into making oppressive, aggressive, possessive and most times, inhumane partisan policies that undermine human rights and destroy human lives! Al of these types of politics are now rife all over the deluded world and have led to the present deplorable living conditions for the majority of mankind to which George belonged because:

Politics thrives on incentives,
Wearing the guise of sham objectives,
Drowning the conscience, selling poise.
Obliterating fairness, bagging the spoils .
Elections are manipulated, often times rigged!
Ballots doctored to favour the rich!
Voters suppressed and their rights ditched,
All subverting Nature's Bills of Rights.

Gerrymandering to swell some polls,
Money speaking louder than the folks.
Dirty hands wash much dirtier hands,...
Candidates shammed'
Candidates slammed!

Parties cremate other parties,
Going to bed with the system,
Not with the people who voted for the system.

All subverting Nature's Bills of Rights!
 To collude and confuse is their motto,
Divide and rule the winning mojo,
Promises made are not delivered,
The electorate left bewildered!
Demagogues feathering their bulging nests,
And the people beat their heavy chests,
Seeming unable to change their fates-

In the face of blatant civil rights rapes.
All subverting Nature's Bills of Right,
Mandatory to all who live their lives
As Likenesses of the Image of God
Without which the affairs of our world
Will increasingly go from bad to worse,
Until we change our loveless course
From force to Love!

Gender Corruption

Gender corruption is as sore to the eye as much as it is to the spirit; not only for *caricaturing* and ridiculing the Omniscience of the Creator in His handiwork, but also for the attempt in forcing arbitrary *external or internal* alterations whatsoever, of the nature and form of what He has permitted to manifest in His perfect structures of all that exists; which each in their different species, is designed specifically for its stipulated purpose of enabling humanity *fulfil* their purpose of earthly incarnation in accordance to His Will!

Of all the creatures in our world, we humans are the only ones that have chosen *to distrust and oppose* this, by wanting to artificially *alter* our gender at will, urged by our intellect, without any reference to the core issue of "*who*" we actually are as spiritual entities in Creation; which sets *boundaries* to the nature of our operations as humans of the specific female and male species *made* so to enable us successfully fulfil that all important spiritual goal we incarnated on earth to do!

Let us honestly agree that there are *noticeable* characteristic differences between the two genders, both in mannerism and appearance that *cannot* be denied. Since nothing happens outwardly in creation that does not have a viable existential connotation, these differences are indelibly hewed into the fabrics of our existence and cannot be altered by a "hair's breath", as said in the aforementioned spiritual book. Our main problems always come from our not looking at things with our spiritual eyes and also therefore not acting likewise!

So when we consider anything that has to do with gender alterations, we need to give it the *full* spiritual attention it deserves, taking into consideration all the ramifications of their karmaic implications in succeeding incarnations on earth or in the beyond! For example, a female who looks and feels like man now, *was* a man who lived and did things like a *woman* in a past life. Come the next life for atonement, what he "*practiced*" becomes *his reality*

Hence, though with a *female organ* now in a *manlike* female body, she still *feels* like a man!

That inner masculinity drives "her" to *desire* a female partner! That's why on the outside, we see a woman attracted to another woman which is described as *lesbianism*! The reverse results in the reaping of homosexuality! This happening has been garnered from the aforementioned one of a kind Spiritual work - "*In The Light of Truth - The Grail Message*", by Abd -ru-shin. It clearly clarifies the phenomenon which has eluded mankind since time began!

It goes on to advise us however, that for his or her spiritual advancement and fulfilment, both sexes should *strongly* resist this urge and the attempt to alter their genders, but to *fight* the urge and remain the masculine or feminine entity he or she now is: Because it is the genuine gender of the spirit's choice, made with the gift of the *free will* at the onset of his or her descent to earth: for the pursuance of the said spiritual goal in the appointed "Earth School", and therefore the *only* one in which he or she is spiritually able to *ever* fulfil his or her life's purpose of existence!

Any alteration therefore jeopardises the offenders chances of survival in the impending cleansing that all human spirits in existence anywhere in creation will experience at the end of this cosmic cycle known as the End Time.

For our own good the aforementioned work lets us know that at this Cosmic Turning point or End Time, the hand of the clock of Cosmic evolution of all matter is close to twelve, meaning that this cycle of world events, that determine our material and spiritual development and maturity will soon close at exactly where it began eons ago, and that a new cycle of *purified* and *spiritualised* life will begin! He lets us know that the purification is occasioned by all the acts of man that are spiritually at variance with the stipulated requirements for the maintenance of cosmic equilibrium in the generation and maintainability of Love, peace and happiness in our world! That is why it is imperative that he or she should now retain the present gender which is his or her original choice at the beginning of his or her incarnations!

A word of caution- Our *free will* may permits us to choose our paths, but the Primordial Natural Laws of Creation without any doubt, will invariably always return the fruit of our decisions to us; determined by the degree to which the decisions acted upon, accord or not with what is expected of a human spirit in training !

We can all easily see how in our taking unconscionable spiritual liberties with our free will doing *only what we want* in flagrant disregard of what would accord with what our Creator Who gave us the "Free Will" demands for *our own good*, has led us to a place of no return in cosmic happenings which the Bringer of the aforementioned Grail Message - "In the Light of Truth" has describes as the "*Cosmic Turning Point*" or the Biblical "*End Time*" of "*reckoning*". This cosmic phenomenon, has auspiciously brought the event of George Floyd's *murder* to the world's subconscious spiritual lamplight, because of it's *nonconformity* to the express Will of God as an approved manner of operation of human spirits, in a world run with no other power but that of His sublime Life Giving, Unconditional Love!

That's why all thee world's shocked spiritual subconscious mind immediately prompted the disapproval of the loveless treatment George Floyd was given!...

It should also enable us to see that the *persistent* misapplication of the power of Love, in the ill-conceived *substitution* of the pervasive a and supreme Omnipotence of God,' with that of the creature *man*; such as i practiced by demagogues and any of the many power wielding individual that exist, like Derek Chauvin and his as mates; contribute to precipitation of the fearful results and many faceted repercussions that now pervades all areas of our daily live!

For instance among other obvious retributions, brought about by our many infringements on the supremacy and governance of the power of Love in our world, enormous agricultural tale telling havocs abound: Unleashing *life* threatening health problems, from the insecticides being applied and the hormones being pumped into the soil which infect the flora and fauna; and now has created food toxic situations in the world! Not less egregious is *cloning* animals for whatever reason, among which is for increasing meat productions for money and fashion. All these abuses of nature, cause us to now and then experience different disasters and catastrophes reciprocally, in the reaction of her various elements that suffer our abusive and *aberrant* inputs into their inherent natural releases of upbuilding radiations for our use. In collision with our destructive radiations released into the atmosphere daily, as farmers continue to pump virgin lands with genetically altered seeds and feeds for bumper yields, contaminating everything we eat and drink; and as we continue to accuse and abuse and maltreat each other in multifarious ways, topped by our wickedness and lovelessness that took George Floyd's and others lives: we continue to ask for retributive consequences rather than rewarding blessings for all our efforts in life!

Medical Corruption

Our agricultural malpractices continue to add to our present deteriorating health conditions which obviously requires us to seek help of the medical institutions. These then heartlessly choose to hold us ransom with their accomplices in the pharmaceutical industries. These giants created to serve humanity with their talents and expertise, unfortunately fail to see the bigger spiritual picture of their callings, once again *distracted* by earthly greed in mainly pursuing financial gains at the cost of precious human lives. This clandestine marrige with the notorious Pharmaceutical giant constellations, which blackmail the desperate sick in hiking prices and making claims for fake medical solutions, is an endemic disease in itself which sends many to their early graves, or making and turning the sick into junkies and human freaks that line our streets or vegetate in our homes! Or getting *racial victims* like George Floyd hooked on the destructive palliative drug that incriminated him!

All this is doubly *aggravated* by the financial nuptial romance contracted between life insurances and health insurances!

Is it any wonder then that our world is largely populated with the endemically sick with diseases of one type or another that could have been easily eradicated with natural remedies which again our greed and self interests, make the rich medical cliques suppress!

The Worship of Money!

We now worship *money* rather than our Creator, allowing it to *totally* control and direct the outcome of everything in our world! We have given it supreme power over our Omniscient Creator who designed and willed everything to come into existence first and foremost, and Whose system is meant to work under the *control* and direction of His Divine loving Laws in the scripted Ten Commandments and replicas in other religions; *monitored* and *assessed* by the primordial natural laws of existence only! This inanimate object "money" *devised* by the little creature man, has now supplanted the life giver Himself Who created man in the first place!!!

In this scenario, it is easy to see why our world has become just as *insensitive* as it's inanimate "master"- *Money*, by our deviating from conducting all our actions with life imbued loving intentions, to the *lifeless* lovelessness and insensitivity of countless deviant natures, characteristic of *lifeless* objects, to which money belongs! Exactly *symbolizing the physical images* formed by the vibrations of our daily activities, for us to utilise and learn from as revealed in the aforementioned Work which lets us know that everything we do, say, or think; takes its symbolic form here on earth or in the world beyond for us to encounter for our continued enlightenment here or our due return to earth for correct spiritual implementation.

That explains why having become as insensitive as an inanimate object, Derek Chauvin was unable to feel nor see that what he was doing to George Floyd was *un-natural!*—

To him and others like him, insensitivity has become natural. This is the attitude of most of humanity right now, which has triggered off the callousness and banditry that now prevails everywhere! It is a state of being in a systemic *trancelike* march towards annihilation, *out of which* our subconscious spiritual selves are being jolted to shake off and return to the true expression of our humanity; by that which transpired on that fateful day of George Floyd's gruesome murder!

If one however decides not to be bothered enough by all the above to do something about it, one then becomes *guilty* of negligence of the duty of a true human spirit, contributing to the swelling band of humanity in the above category of *destructive* rather than upbuilding participant in our spiritual developmental mission, pertinent above all for the continued preservation of all life especially at this crucial "End Time" of *sieving and reckoning*!

We can all conclusively discern that the continued pursuit of money and power in the same callous and obsessive manner, is indeed the "root of all the evil" that is Choking mankind with the iron grip that has turned nations against nations, factions against factions, villages against each other, brother against brothers, and sisters the same. Neighbours against neighbours and all because of *money*! Children turn against parents, business against business, governments against the people, the world *against* itself! With one aim alone making more money at all costs!...

Is it not high time that we realised that we have become *enslaved* by money which compels us to do only what it wants, destroying our will to conform to the Will of He who made us all including the *tool* of money itself ? Is it not most likely that the fear of loosing faces with their commander and consequently their money earning law enforcement jobs, that made Derek Chauvin's mates become accomplices in that murderous act committed against George Floyd? We work for money from night till dawn. We kill for money, lie for money every hour everyday, no matter what may be at stake! We sell our lives, our children our pride, our morals, even our faiths, for the spiritual *crippling* commodity! - -

Our abilities to act as expected of us have even further become completely hampered in this respect by the conduct of *bankers*, who illegally *swell* their portfolios by encouraging us to invest our earnings in their banks, to gain *inflated* returns, with their adept employment of various deviant gimmicks even including money laundering, counterfeiting currencies and inflating given service interests! These epitomise the evils of dishonesty and greed no expected nor desirable of any practicing and sincere humane organisations committed to honouring the All-Holy Will of the Creator of all things! Further more, the control of money over our lives has so *overshadowed* that of our Creator's, that the envious leadership of the political affairs of our world is determined by factoring in the highest *economic status* of the country of choice; not by factoring in the status or standard of her overall *spiritual* development, which should be the only factor for assessing such a global leadership among the spiritual beings that we are!....

To achieve this prestigious esteem of all the other nations of the world, each country's leadership devices policies that will help them attain the highest global financial status, but underplays that which would enable his or her people attain the aforementioned spiritual goal! In this money oriented *mismanagement* of our lives, the leaders focus all attention on all the money making policies he or she and her supporters can devise to boost the economy, even if it means the lenders driving the investors into insolvency with the stigma of bankruptcies. While the treasuries, their working counterparts, using the powerful whips of the land, levy taxes for spurious ends, which end up being poured down their private financial draining networks. In this overloaded and complex money oriented frenzy, loopholes are invariably created which enable the tax returners to make false claims at the end of the year. While Insurance companies capitalise on our fears and make life insurances become "*debt*" incurrences; with the companies easily refuting their sworn assurances in the contracts, turning deaf ears to financially uneducated clients, litigating them with counter claims.

It is easy to see that this obsessive economy driven life of which we are all guilty, is a tempestuous preoccupation that demands our serious immediate attention!

Corruption also nestles in corporations like a snake, slithering through the corporate ladder with the CEOs doing whatever it may take to rake in more gains. They *bribe* politicians and lobby legislators for personal gains. All taking place at the *consumers expense*, mindless of the law of what you sow you must reap now or in the next life! These giant money gorging corporations do not stop at intimidating competitors but revel in making *nefarious* deals that satisfy their greed; cooking their books to pay less taxes than their cooks. They claim tax exemptions, concessions and privileges for their philanthropic companies, some of which do not even exist! All against the nature of those made in the likeness of the Image of God and should only live *righteously* in every way.

All world's religions, civil and social advancement institutions were originally founded for no other reason than for helping us do that, when we were still spiritually connected and hence attuned to receiving the pure and clear uninhibited promptings of our spiritual tool of the intuitions! Now that all world's leaders vie for the possession of nuclear power for warfare, while ignoring the needs of their people, shows how spiritually disconnected and dead we have indeed become: highlighted by the daily events of rampant shootings on streets, schools, pavilions, churches and synagogues; punctuated by the brutal murders of such as Briana Taylor, George Floyd and many others!

But that such an event took place even before the camera on that fateful day for everyone to see, does not only give us hope, but offers us an important wake-up call, to make our human identity caps bear the shining *spiritual* logos of universal *unconditional life preserving* Love! We can easily accomplish this by deciding to: -

Give rather than take,
Forgive rather than revenge.
Support rather than suppress.
Encourage rather than discourage.
Cooperate rather than terrorise:
Inspire rather than deride.
Praise rather than disparage .
Trust rather than distrust.

Respect rather than suspect.
Integrate rather than segregate.
Restrain rather than instigate.
Liberate rather than enslave.

Admire rather than detest.

Include rather than exclude.

Placate rather than incense.

Liberate rather than oppress!

Protect rather than abuse.

Love rather than hate !

Preserve rather than destroy.

Save rather than kill!

Share rather than monopolise.

Befriend rather than antagonise.

Cause laughter rather than tears.

In the eyes of all of the human race! -

So that as human spirits who are made in the Likenesses of the Image of God, Whose benevolent acts are inexhaustible, and as *like attracts its own kind,* Love will play its natural role of letting Love attract Love once more in the hearts of rulers, masters and servants, the hearts of the woman and of the man - *The hearts of all humankind!*

This is because in the process of our developing to become the human Likenesses of the Image of God, we are eternally supported by the fact that *all things* that are created out of the bellowing ocean of light from the Love of our Creator-God, are endowed with the essence of the Creator's inexhaustible Divine power of Love with which we are to *operate* in all of Creation! That is why *nothing* else but that Living Sublime Love, that Life Giving and sustaining Love, is the proven antidote for all the wrongs in the entire universe! Hence: —

When we do anything

Without Love as the motive power:

We put our lives in danger.

We play with scorching fire.

We break the only hammer

That gives form to all there is.

When we do anything

Without Love as the motive power,
Our world falls apart,
Cause we fail to play our harps
And wear the angelic crown
Of the Living God's Image!
When we do anything
Without Love as the motive power,
We counterfeit the love in us,
Break the bond
Distort the norm.-

And butchered the love in us
When we do anything
Without Love as the motive poer,
In the crypt of hate
Crypt of greed,
Crypt of prejudice spiced with villainy
We cremate the love in us;
In the crypt of hate,
Crypt of greed ,
Crypt of prejudice spiced with vice!

When we do anything
Without Love as the motive power,
We confound the Love in us,!
Contorted the Love in us!
Debased the Love in us!
Demean the Love in us !
Disfigure the Love in us !

But Loving others as we love ourselves -
Breaks the tension,
Sets in motion all
Life's vibrations.
Smooths all frictions,
Empowers our actions
With the nectar of our essence.
Cause Love alone has all the gifts
For all humanity's needs
In cities or hamlets,
Villages or palaces,
Private or public places
All Institutions around the globe!....

Let us then wake up from our deadening spiritual sleep of vicious *self-complacency* and make the necessary decision to *obey* God our Maker, by living our lives with the loving energy with which He made us in the first place, for nothing else will work!

It is the only thing that will forestall the acceleration of our imminent collapse, for we are now poised at the tipping edge of the precipice, in the reckoning of cosmic happenings!

Not long ago, the UN announced that our world is now in the "code RED" condition, echoing the Biblical predictions of impending catastrophic happenings ahead! It is therefore deemed necessary for us *reverse* our vibrational output of *destructive* energies in whatever form, by transmitting the only energy that is not so in all its ramifications, but is lovingly constructive, purifying and benevolent by sharing:

The love that-hears all,
Not just some people.
Love that listens to all,
Not just to some people.

Love that gives to all,
Not just to some people.
Love that stands by all,
Not just by some people.

Love that speaks good of all,
Not only of some people.
Love that cares for all
Not only for some people.

Love that protects all
Not only some people.
Love that defends all,
Not any special ones.

Love that provides for all,
Not any special ones.
Love that helps all,
Not any special ones.

Love that believes all,
Not just some people.
That cooperates with all,
Not any preferred ones.

Love that values all,
Not just the special ones.
That does what is good for all,
Not just for the special ones.

That empathises with all,
Not with some people.

That is kind to everyone,
Not just the chosen ones.

Love that thinks well of everyone,
Not just the chosen ones.
That sees only what is good in everyone,
Not just in the chosen ones.

Love that provides for everyone,
Not just for some people
That empowers everyone,
Not just the chosen ones.

That respects everyone,
Not just the chosen ones.
That makes all happy,
Not just some chosen ones.

Love that rewards everyone,
Not just some people.
That loves all without exception,
In the likeness of the Acts of God !

But alas since the "Fall of Man" through Adam and Eve, we have not synchronised nor harmonised with God's governing symphony of sublime Love; but brutally scrambled, caricatured, *jarred* and perverted all His intensions in the cacophony of our continued evil engagements! This cacophonous cosmic music we now play has perjured our souls by distorting our lives, forcing us to expect only all the wrong outcomes from our cacophonous daily inputs into the power stream of existence, which can only give us back what we have put into it in compliance to the *irrevocable* law of *What you sow you must reap*"! Hence the chaos that now reigns in all regions of the world! - -

Judging that "Love governs all existence" as revealed in the exceptiona spiritual work "In The Light of Truth - The Grail Message" by Abd Ru Shin the aforementioned one of a kind work in existence that explains all that wa hitherto unknown about our Creator and us human spirits, a work tha emphatically proves that *God is "Love" itself*, and therefore all tha manifested and still manifest out of Him are made out of His outpoured Love energy; it stands to reason to reiterate that Love is what composes everything created right to the atoms of the cells of everything in our universe! We cannot exist nor ever do anything successfully anytime without it!

Any seeker for the truth about our existence and how everything i supposed to work in creation after going through the content of this book can obtain the said special spiritual work from the Alexander Bernhard publishing USA on Amazon, from the website of http:/.www.alexander bernhardt.us/. .It will go along way to clarifying our nagging unsolved mysteries of life and remove our doubts and hesitations in making the righ choices, provided they are guided by our intuitions!

Going through the work opens one's mind to the knowledge and observation of occurrences in the community and the world at large, making one come to realise the following: That without the constant interchange o this energy of Love from one entity to another in whatever the position o location, whatever the time or condition, whatever the problem o circumstance, whatever the relationship or association, the organisation religious or political affiliation, institution or industry; without this crucia interchange, things invariably go wrong! Human lives degenerate as we ar witnessing acts of insensitivity and lovelessness that are manifest i behaviours such as that of police officers who accost, arrest and murder th likes of George Floyd Or randomly harassing innocent people for show o power!

Since no one was originally born devoid of the endowment of the essenc of *pure sublime love*, it is important to remind ourselves that to have no become such *loveless* human beings, predominantly obsessed with the *carn* love and money; is detrimental to our *spiritual growth*: because it exto *physical* rather than upbuilding sublime *Love* of *benevolent* service to on *another*, making it a wasteful application of the power of Love in us! And b perpetrating this physical -preference, we obviously demonstrate our failure in yet another aspect of our lives which also needs our well considered attention, because it is an area in which women are very much the cardinal motivating participants!

Womanhood plays the role of guardianship in the maintainance of mankind's spiritual connection with the Creator, in the purity and sensitivity of her being. Her delicate receptive structure, lends hand to the heightening of her intuitive faculty with which she does so. This is one of the reasons why the role of womanhood in the whole of Creation was made indispensable by the Creator; and where she has woefully failed to live up to expectations, at the expense of all mankind!

All the condemnable acts of mankind that now prevails, regrettably stem from that most undeniable painful fact that human *womanhood*, of all creatures, has so far failed to live up to the truth that " *to whom much is given, much is expected*" -

The woman of creation, as revealed in the one of a kind spiritual only book, was and remains the one who the Creator gave the sacred gift of the *sensitivity* of her intuition, to enable her readily to receive spiritual guidance from above for her required nurturing of all humanity; to prepare them for their spiritual development in creation! But due to her failure to fulfil this duty, by irresistibly succumbing to all forms of temptations by the *watchful darkness*, through the enticement of all that is material, easily as conceived by the usurping intellect; the emanating radiations there from which block her intuitive reception of the indispensable spiritual guidance: mankind's Divinely all-holy Willed spiritual development has been generally and sadly left in the hands of earth-men, who are not *specifically gifted* or equipped to do so by the Creator! —It is not unlikely that the chaotic and disastrous state of human affairs we are all witnessing, is the outcome of womanhood's *spiritual* nurturing having been left in the hands of the *spiritually* unqualified candidatures of earthmen!

Consider, is this not why "A Nation Under God" and all other nations of our world whose rulerships are not guided by the advices of their females, have consistently failed to guide their citizens to the only path that will fulfil

God's All-Holy Will on the *earth school* He created for us to do so? Being bereft of the much needed influence of true womanhood, our leaders are left to establish laws and policies that leave out the spiritual components of governance. Is it therefore of any surprise that such inhuman and spiritually unacceptable acts as stifling their fellow human spirits to death, the way they did to George Floyd, or conducting acts of wars, genocides and all forms of aggression on other nations which are completely *objectionable*, and which spiritually oriented upbringing by the spiritual being-"*the woman*", would have brought to be is now the norm? It is also the basis of the highly intellectual structure of all our educational systems which are biased toward the deluding dominance of intellectual and gross *material* development rather than spiritual development! A situation that has amplified much of the condemnable discriminatory and superiority complexes and attitudes of the materially so called intellectually accomplished people of the world, against their wrongly assumed illiterate and materially unaccomplished *backward* unfettered counterparts, who have remained human spirits that are unadulterated or affected by all the misguiding ploys of the intellectual manoeuvres of the materially oriented world!

Bear in mind the aforementioned scientific affirming evidence of the research done on the sad effect of higher education on the spirituality of the ambitious misled "victims"!

The Failure Of Womanhood

My fellow women, permit me to reiterate that to us, so much was indeed given by the Giver of life, that if we only knew the *stupendous* magnitude of this gift; we would do everything in our power to *obey* Him in gratitude for that awesome gift! Don't take my word for it but refer to an eye opening lecture that explains what we women are supposed to be doing on earth and what we ought not to be doing for the preservation of the power of that gift in the lecture titled- "The Woman of Subsequent Creation ", in the afore-mentioned work— "In The Light of Truth - The Grail Message" by Abd-ru-shin.

In it you will find out how privileged and special we women are! You will find out that the Creator gave us women the possession of a special ability, as said before, by clothing our spirits with the gift of our *delicate* but *powerful* intuition, for the express purpose of making us more receptive to His promptings as said. This was to make us much more easily able to gain access to Him for *spiritual* help "*in its purity*" for our duties as would-be mothers, thereby entrusting us with the Divine duty of being the *Priestesses of Purity*, which empowers us to nurture all humanity in spiritual purity and love, both which are of utmost importance in creation and inseparable from His all Holy Will!

Men don't have this gift. They have other divine gifts but not this very awesome one, of controlling what spiritually transpires in the entire world, through the way we nurtured the seeds of humanity *spiritually*!

Is this not the highest responsibility and honour that has been bestowed on any creature!?- -

When we look around the entire world today however, especially to the horrific events in past ages and now, the escalation of devastations, caused by recent wars in Europe and Asia; and other acts of man's inhumanity to his fellow man: brought home to everyone by the event of the murder of George Floyd and others; can we say that we have done a good job with our most awesome gift? Our seeds *continue* to engaged in all manners of nefarious activities, that clearly indicate that we have not lived up to our spiritual unique responsibility! The unavoidable question then, is how did we women fail in our God given duty? How could we have prevented George Floyd's gruesome murder or any murders at all?

You see fellow women, that we are so gracefully and very delicately structured both spiritually and physically, indicates that we are expected to display qualities of delicate *purity* and grace in everything we say, think and do! For The Almighty speaks and instructs us through the intrinsic nature and naturalness of everything in His creation: Making life a very delicate and purely spiritual material, which must be handled *delicately* and in *purity*, and in an all embracing delicate manner and form. Therefore, since the management of our lives is said to be spiritually in the hands of women, we have to be the true embodiments of that element of sublime sensitive *delicacy and purity* in every way.

Are we? Let us take stock:—

We emulate men who are differently structured in nearly everything especially in clothing these days! How delicate is that?

We emulate men in career choices!

We emulate men in mannerisms and gestures. We emulate men in sport of all kinds etc., etc.!

Are men delicate? Those who appear to be are given unsavoury names.

We emulate men in our intellectual pursuits which drive the physical world only through the employment of the gifts given particularly to men claiming that what men can do women can equally do... Really?

Nature refutes and dismisses this claim, for if it were true, we would have been built to look physically the same!—

In the course of all these claims, we have not only succeeded in replacing our delicateness with the coarseness of men, whose nature is given to having the complementary element of physical strength and boldness, for the duties they too have to perform in Creation; but have also become susceptible to the *hybridisation* of the spiritual vibrations and radiations of most of us women who are guilty of the above *distorting* inclinations!

This among other inhibiting effects of other none-feminine practices, has most certainly led to our *inability* to continue to connect with the higher power, for the reception of the most necessary spiritual guidance we need, in order that we can successfully carry out the sacred delicate duty of nurturing mankind spiritually, which is only to be achieved with that special intuitive ability that was graciously given to all womanhood! —

The Bringer of the said living word of God for the salvation of mankind at this close of the cycle of all world events, further discloses that, by being the unwavering *Priestess of Purity*, womanhood would open a *pure* Divine channel for humanity to be able to maintain the *desire* to know and *only do* the holy Will of God; making her the fitting *"Guardian of the Flame for Holy Longing"*- the longing to doing only what is good for all of mankind: and not to ever be the obstinate and perpetually noncompliant agents of disloyalty and wilful disobedience that we have now become!

If as women, we had lived our lives as *Priestesses of Purity* the twin essence of Love, this aberration would not have taken place, because all our actions would have been *spiritually* guided; and people like George Floyd would be alive today! This clearly confirms the fact that contrary to all Divine expectations, womanhood has allowed herself to be lured to failure, by perpetrating the Adam and Eve syndrome of falling into sundry material temptations; one of which is her false desire to please the man, among other distracting illusions, choosing—

To loose her divination role even more,
In the uncouth game of strip and show!
Everywhere are popping bare breasts
And long enticing bare legs,
With eyelashes like the wings of birds,
And painted claws for finger nails!

Making her a play toy with no soul -
Stuffed with mouthwatering sex treats,
Dancing to the male like a puppet on a string.

The priceless priestess reduced to a clown
In a world that has thrown away her crown!
Fouling her saintly brows,
In a world without the sense of shame.
Bringing her down from her throne,
Clouding her sacred sight and role;
Making her a mouse in a cage of cats:
Devouring her piece by piece, flesh by flesh,
With dripping mouthfuls of gushing lust!

Befogging the world with infectious dusts
Arising from her spiritual crash,
By turning decorum into trash,
In a world without the sense of shame,
But totally disgraced
And riddled with grief,
All nations lacking peace
And full of hate and greed -
But Love will always heal!

Will turn man around
From all that keeps him bound
To self destruction and delusions.
Bound to nihilistic acts of brutality
Indolence and spiritual death.
Comatose in denial,

Of his impending doom:

Unless he turns away soon,

From the material power loom

The fact that we are *dual* entities walking on earth, made of the *invisible* spirit that reincarnates over and over again in the acquired suitable tool of the *visible* human bodies of different descriptions, in order to finally complete our spiritual only assignment on earth; the one spiritual and the other corporeal, the former immortal, the latter mortal: Requires us to seriously pay more attention to what the spirit needs for its eternal existence! But that spiritual need has been totally disregarded in our lives, leaving our spirit uncared for like a homeless orphan, roaming the world that has rejected its indisputable contribution to all that goes on all around it; without which mankind's efforts for true progress in the Divinely approved directions will *never* be achieved! —

This continued spiritual destructive condition that has prevailed over mankind for thousands of years is now being brought to book in the final reckoning of the End Time, under the rule of the long promised judgement of "The Son of Man", Who is the *executive* Will of God! He being the *incarnate* "Holy Spirit" of God *in flesh* as the Lord Jesus Christ was the *personification* of the "Love" of God in flesh! He, Jesus, promised the coming of the *Son of Man* to the disciples, using "HE" not "it" in reference to Emanuel or Immanuel- the "God *with us*", not He Jesus Himself; Who will come to "judge the world of sin and righteousness. He was *duly born* on earth just like Jesus was, to complete the representation of the composition of the *Holy Trinity* working in Creation- God the Father-God the Son- God the Holy Spirit! —

I was humbly awed with the unexpected privilege of having the sacred image of this embodiment of the Creative Will power of God, radiated to me on three occasions in dreams, where His composite embodiment of the executive image of the Divine Power of Justice, Love and Purity was projected in the sky, in three episodes of very lucid dreams in full colour, more than twenty years ago! In the first episode in 1983, He gradually emerged from the farthest edge of the horizon in an immaculate, voluminous shimmering white robe, with a covering over his invisible face on an equally *immaculate* white stallion, *majestically* riding across and covering the entire heavens from one end to the other, top to bottom; posturing *invincibility* across the entire sky- holding a white whip! (Of JUDGEMENT, - my interpretation). The magnificent regal figure in the blue sky grew larger and larger, covering the entire sky as it quietly zoomed towards my bewildered gaze and then slowly and silently vanished!!!....

In the second episode two years later in 1985, He, the Will of God made man, our Lord Emanuel, permitted the projection of His Image in the sky once again in yet another very vivid lucid full coloured dream appearing in an invincible powerful and mighty awe inspiring submarine that slowly emerged behind and rose above all the buildings on the surface of the earth spanning from horizon to horizon!

When it stopped rising, the central projection of the submarine slowly parted and transformed into a rosey radiant triangle in which He appeared as an ageless, all knowing, fresh and delicate youth, steadily looking inspiringly down at me without uttering a sound or a word for the entire time that felt like eternity; then all slowly and silently vanished again! —

I immediately woke up and wrote down all what I had been permitted to receive, just as I did after the first episode.

In the third episode, the same night, I was transported to the mountain of salvation in old biblical mount Hebron, now the location of the headquarters of the Grail Movement on Earth; the only place where the Holy power of the Almighty is now anchored on earth and where He, the *Son of Man* and the *Bringer and author* of " In The Light of Truth - The Grail Message"... lived and wrote the book. There He instructed me and three other ladies in attendance in the anteroom of His abode to fit "*the jigsaw puzzle of life*" among other assignments. —

After *twenty years* of observing and examining all aspects of our lives, in their demonstrable natural occurrences, and the common characteristic they all posses; juxtaposing each life occurrence with the mechanism of the working out of the Will of God in Creation: All the puzzle pieces fitted and bore witness to being manifestations of different aspects of the Divine *Love* energy particles of God's essence everything; having *originated* from Him

Who is Love!

These findings concretised and *validated* the fact that Love is the core essence or the only energy material with which the particles of all the atoms, down to the minutest sub-atomic denominations of everything in our bodies and in all of creation is made! They being the measure and contents of everything that exists, logically makes Love the only energy with which we are to be operating in our everyday activities, not only in this world but in all Creation.

In fulfilment of my dream/vision assignment, I have since published all that I was able to find out in a book entitled "The Love That We Are" with a sub title of " Our True Identity."

(To be purchased from Amazon and Barnes and Nobles).

In my 20 years research and in-depth observations of natural occurrences as stated above and continuing, I have found out that the *absence* of Living Love in our relationships, in thought, words and actions, lead to the malfunctioning of the mechanism that galvanises all agents of creation in their respective harmonious operations, right to the atomic and subatomic level. This demands our reciprocally expected constant compliance to God's All Holy Will, for the maintenance of harmony in the mechanism of Creation!

When we don't, the atoms of the cells in our bodies and that composing all of nature, invariably react unfavourably; causing all manners of illnesses, and in our environments, causing all forms of what we term natural disasters!....

We cannot therefore continue to ignore any of these, because our world is now tottering at the brink of its final collapse! It is also the reason why the wakeup call given to us by the events of the murders of George Floyd, Briana Taylor and others should be headed.

"Spiritual Life Matters" a great deal!

Conclusion

George Floyd's Mission Karma will *bear no fruit* for mankind if after all that transpired during and after the horrendous event, humanity *fails* to join him to:

Let Love Lead the way
In everything we do every day
From dawn till night,
Jumpstarting Love's active might
Within the spirit of the child;
That he or she, fully armed
Embrace the world with open arm!

Will bear no fruit:
If we fail
To let Love Lead the way,
In communities every day!
To shunhate,
But plant Love.
Banish xenophobia and race-o-phobia!

Homophobia and zoophobia,
Negrophobia and kainotophobia,
Europhobia and Afrophobia
Acrophobia and Numerophobia
Francophjobia and anglophobia
Aquaphobia and anthrophobia

rachnophobia and all the phobias!

To fruit if we fail
to Let Love Lead the way
n businesses:
To eradicate greed and exploitation,
aggrandisement and deception,
Dispossession of the have nots,
or the benefit of the have much!

To fruit
if we fail
to Let Love Lead the way
n governance everywhere!
for equality and equity,
Clemency in policies
With integrity and honesty

Will bear no fruits
if we fail:
To want rest in peace!
And set compassion free
To reign with of Living Love .
Rendering poverty out of touch,
n the Will of Almighty God!

No fruit if we fail
to let Love Lead the Way
n law enforcement everywhere!
Banishing megalomaniac clowns,
That Justice may wear the crown
Of true humanity,;

Not champion sheer cruelty.

No fruits if we fail
To Let Love Lead the Way -
Cremating despondency
In man's Love phoenix
Hand in hand with Living love.
That rules the entire universe!

Love to lead everywhere
No matter who we are,
No matter what we are,
No matter where we've been,
No matter where we want to be,
No matter our creed,
Nor our breed!

Love to Lead the Way
In childhood and adulthood.
Adventurous youths
Or the Corporate employer,
The mentor and benefactor.

Fail to share the Love we receive
Every split second of the day,
From the Lord of all creation -
God the Father Almighty,
The Creator of the universe,
Omniscient, Omnipresent, Omnipotent,
For all eternity!

Fail to share the Love received

Every split second of the day,
From the Lord of all creation -
God the Father Almighty,
The Creator of the universe;
Omniscient, Omnipresent, Omnipotent
For all eternity!

Fail:
To let Love be the only way
So war will be no more
Terrorism will be no more.
Homicide will be no more.
Crimes will be no more .
Corruption will be no more.
Bigotry will be no more
Prejudice will be no more

Greed will be no more
Exploitation will be no more
Egotism will be no more.
Nepotism will be no more.
Despotism will be no more.
Dictatorship will be no more .
Vanity will be no more.

Selfishness will be no more.
Exploitation will be no more.
Slavery will be no more .
Warfare will be no more - - -
And Love will rule the world!

EPILOGUE

On a more personal note, let me share these experiences that I have ha of the workings of the power of Love on levels that reveal the unchangeabl sublimity and pervasiveness of its mechanism, demonstrating its universalit in execution for the prescribed maintenance of harmony in all Creation tha is governed only by the invincible power of Living Love. I am sure you ma have had some yourself.

I had a potted plant in Evanston Illinois, of blooming beautiful hibiscu in our living room. Every year its beauty was marred by disturbing pests c fruit flies that loved the nectar of the flowers. In my ignorance and concern I bought "Raids" and angrily attacked the poor things to get rid of them Indeed, they would die of the poison to my great relief that season but, woul promptly return in time in the next!

It took me three seasons of despair to then realise that I was going again the law of Love for my fellow creatures in our world! I had no right to tak their lives! They too had the right to live and enjoy the gift from th benefactor, our God! So, I appealed to the loving nature beings that take ca of all nature as revealed in the one of a kind Spiritual work - "*In The Ligh of Truth - The Grail Message*", to handle the situation in accordance wit the All-holy Will of the giver of *all life*. In three days or so, the sweet-toothe or sweet-tongued flies were gone and never came back again in any season!–

At another occasion I was chatting with a neighbour by our apartmer car park in Skokie, Illinois when a wasp zoomed between us and menacing buzzed around the neighbour about two feet away from me, who wa frantically flapping and flagging it to chase it away! I intervened and aske her to remain calm to dissipate the vibration and radiation of her infectio fear and agitation, which was disturbing the wasp's sensitivity to any infusio of disturbing vibrations in the should be serene natural state of harmonious peace and Love that it understands!

She stopped her disturbing actions and the wasp finally swooped by me and buzzed away!

At another occasion, a group of us were clearing a bush for the building of our Temple of The Grail Movement in Atlanta. We paused for lunch sitting on a bench in the clearing. Behold a swarm of insects came rolling across forming a conical shape before us, and about three feet away and above us. I gently told them to withdraw into the interior of the forest where they would find adequate and suitable nourishment other than the ones we were having. They heard me because they promptly swung round back into the forest and out of sight!

Half an hour or so later, the co-crossbearer who was sitting next to me and saw the insects in the first encounter, nudged me and said: "Hey look, your friends have now gone to trouble the children at their lunch (sitting in the clearing ten feet or so to our right), better talk to them again and send them away from the children". I gently raised my voice and told them what I had said before. To our delight and gratitude, they did and never returned to trouble any of us again!

On the 23rd of November, 2018, a friend and I were waiting in someone's living room to be given a ride to a party. A young girl was trying to stop a medium size grey dog from coming at us! I asked the girl to let the dog be. The dog gingerly went to sniff at my friend sitting next to me on the sofa, then he or she turned to do the same to me. He/she repeated this action then came closer to me and raised its left paw and placed it gently on my right knee and looked up at me...!

I have always loved animals and have had pets of guinea pigs, dogs, cats, sparrow and a parrot many years ago but don't now. So, I told the dog that understood him as I stroked its head. Then it raised both fore-legs and gently placed them on my knees still looking at me, raising its head very close to my face. I held his head and stroked it, telling him I totally understood his gesture and shared its understanding of that which binds us all as creatures made with and driven by nothing else but by the energy and sublime power of God's Love! The dog slowly withdrew with his or her attendant.

If Love can do all the foregoing to the interaction between man and animals and other creatures in existence, how much more with us human spirits!

Love is the common denominator in life for all existence and the only viable living power that can unite all mankind to live harmoniously with one another in the fulfilment of our common destiny of achieving spiritual maturity in every way and ennobling our environments in the Holy Will of God; hence the only weapon for combating all the evil in our beleaguered world, preventing events like that which took George Floyd and others lives!

This work is in honour of George Floyd's subconscious brave accomplishment of his "Mission Karma". All the other fellow human spirit who have been murdered in the brutal manners we all see daily, may have been killed for other karmaic reasons which are not "Mission" oriented, but nevertheless not of *less importance* in the fulfilment of our shared existence. Not necessarily being *Mission Karmas* could be why none of them have had the impact and attention that George Floyd's case prompted round the world.

His murder *raised* this much brows and took this much hair raising turn most likely because, we are now *totally oblivious* of the recurring fact of *reincarnation* in the march of our spiritual evolution. We have also lost the knowledge that crucial supportive events are envisaged and *planned* in advance in the ethereal part of creation; hence his preplan for the "Mission Karma" in question. So it was *spiritually* designed that his death should be widely viewed round the world in real time of the news media's presence in the area, *auspiciously* to be prompted by the presence of the Law enforcement officers appearance and activities in the precinct. Not only that!

That there would be an audience to witness and subsequently report it as it was so done by the young girl member of that audience who recorded the event in her mobile phone! —

None of the previous atrocities of this nature was ever given this much in-depth publicity and attention in recent memory! Those others have served other spiritual purposes, most of which the agitations about the horrific events however fell on deaf ears of the general public, although they continue o expose the endemic unacceptable prevalent practices of our biased political, legal and social systems!

But the dastardly murder of poor George Floyd on that fateful day, was aimed *exceptionally at opening* our hearts and eyes to the problems which now need our urgent attention, *If we truly want to continue to exist in God's Love based Creation*! Let us do this now!

Thank you for your patience!

NOTE

Anyone who would like to fully understand his or her life and the reason why he or she and everything exists, to also come to know how the world really came about, despite the suppositions of scientists and the story of creation in the Bible or other religious books, but to truly get to know how it all actually happened and Who God really is, What He is and of what He is made, Where He is and how His power operates in the entire universe He created, of what the universe and everything in it, including human beings and animals are made and much more about all existence; needs to simply look for all the enlightenment he or she may ever desire about these nagging life issues, from the never before indisputable living facts revealed in the one of a kind spiritual work

-

"In The Light of Truth - The Grail Message" by Abd-ru-shin Published by Alexander Publishing USA website: http. // www.alexander-bernhardt.us/

Thanks again!